One Man's Compassion

Fulton Buntain
Hal Donaldson

One Man's Compassion

Fulton Buntain
and Hal Donaldson

Copyright © 1989
by the Calcutta Mission of Mercy
Printed in the United States of America
ISBN: 0-88368-214-1

Scripture quotations are taken from the *New King James Version.* Copyright © 1979, 1980, 1982, Thomas Nelson Inc., Publishers.

Dedication

Dedicated to the Reverend John Edward Southard and his wife, Alice, for their unselfish, dedicated, and prayerful support of the ministry of Mark and Huldah Buntain.

Acknowledgement

Special thanks to B. W. Corpany, Solomon and Lori Wang, Judy Ermold, Scott Craven, Cherisse Jackson, Donald and Dorothy Waggoner, Steve and Becky Donaldson, David and Kristy Donaldson, Paul and Susan Peissner, Betty and Bernie Foote, Roland and Reahn Hubin, Vern and Martha Kingsland, Daryl Perna, Joe Perna, Lisa Rich, Karen Kingsland, Ray and Barbara Horwege, Doug and Judi Schultz, Jack Allen, Norman Arnesen, Ken Horn, Larry Rust, and Terry Toliver.

Heartfelt appreciation to Doug Wead and Doree Donaldson.

Authors' Note

Some names have been changed and events altered at the authors' discretion. Many of the descriptions of India are accounts made prior to the present government's rise to power. India has made great strides in recent years.

Dr. and Mrs. Buntain with their special friend, Mother Teresa.

Forewords

Whenever we visited Mark Buntain and the Calcutta Mission of Mercy Hospital, the doors were always open. I am very grateful to all the people there who have shared in the joy of loving by sharing their time, their hands, so altogether we can do something beautiful for God.

Mother Teresa
Sisters of Charity

I never knew Francis of Assisi, but I knew his spiritual descendent, Mark Buntain. Here's a man, who, with his wife, left all to follow Jesus and to minister to the poorest in His name. God did mighty things through this man and his ministry.

Pat Boone

Mark Buntain was one of those rare Christian men who totally poured out his life in ministering to the needs of the multitudes of God's beloved needy. Anyone reading about the power of the love of God in this man's life will be richly blessed.

Roger W. Jepsen
Former U.S. Senator, Iowa

One Man's Compassion, story by story, with truth stranger than fiction, reminds us of a desperate world, so needy that only God's love demonstrated in caring hands can overcome it.

John Ashcroft
Governor of Missouri

I have had the privilege of meeting many of the missionaries in the world. No one impressed me more than Mark Buntain. For thirty-four years he sacrificially gave of himself to the people of Calcutta for Christ's sake.

Literally hundreds of thousands have been fed, clothed, and educated by the ministry of this man. My hat goes off to him, especially since he ministered in Calcutta, perhaps the most impoverished city in the world with its teeming millions and indescribable filth.

From the time he began this work until his recent death, Mark and his wife Huldah lived in the same small apartment they secured thirty-four years ago. To me, Mark was a modern day George Muller, a spiritual hero. He exemplified faithfulness to one's calling, persistence, dependability, compassion, and complete selflessness. Mark Buntain's life reflected how Jesus would be ministering in the world today.

Mark Buntain persistently lived both aspects of the walk with Christ relative to others: outreach and social concern. What a model he has been for so many of us! Therefore it is more than a pleasure to write a preface for this book. It is my honor.

Franklin Graham
Director of Samaritan's Purse
and World Medical Missions

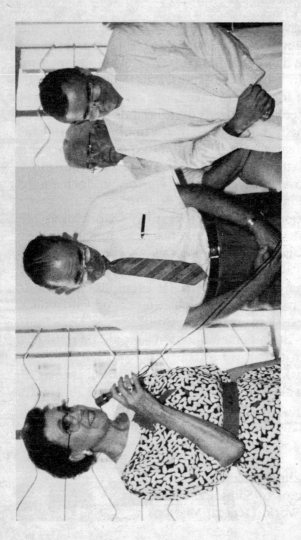

Mark's sister, Alice Southard, Mark Buntain, and his brother, Fulton Buntain, together in Calcutta in 1986.

Contents

Introduction

In 1983 I was invited to have lunch with missionary legend Mark Buntain, who had given more than thirty years of his life to the people of Calcutta, India.

I had read accounts of Calcutta's poverty and filth, but my skeptical journalistic nature led me to label the articles as embellished, graphic literature meant to strum the sympathetic chords of even the hardest heart. "Surely Calcutta is more than rats, starving children, and rabid dogs," I told myself. "These writers merely centered on the unsightly side of Calcutta. There must be the 'other side of the tracks.'" Mark Buntain must have sensed my ignorance. One afternoon he invited my wife and me to visit Calcutta to see for ourselves.

A year later we stepped off a Thai Airlines DC-10 into the world of *The Compassionate Touch*. I was no longer a reader, a philosopher. I had become a participant. No longer could I rationalize my lack of involvement. The sights evoked in me the same pain I had felt when my father was killed in an automobile accident seventeen years earlier.

As we exited the terminal, we trudged through a multitude of brown-skinned boys and girls whose dark, somber eyes seemed to be asking if we would be "today's savior." Their bare feet were archless, calloused, and ridden with sores. The monsoon displayed no pity on them. Raindrops glanced off their shaven heads with bruising force. I later learned their hair was cut short to fight the infestation of lice. Their T-shirts and cut-offs showed evidence of having battled the monsoon many times before, nights spent unshielded from the rains and winds. Their eyes were penetrating, hoping this white man would reach into his pocket. They all knew what that meant. Outstretched hands and arms obstructed our path to the taxi. Some were begging for an offering that would ensure survival; others reached to touch us as if we were royalty.

The taxi ride through the city in a battered, beige sedan reminded me of a fast-paced bumper car attraction. Our driver, Mujib, was a modern day Houdini, escaping snares in the traffic without using his brakes. The thought crossed my mind, I hope he *has* brakes. My wife sunk her nails into my pant leg as our Indy 500 driver raced his rattling vehicle through a maze of bicycles, rickshaws, pedestrians, dogs, cows, buses, and cars.

Off the side of the road, a naked baby was drinking from what appeared to be a coffee can. He then poured its contents over his head. The black water made his hair darker. A suffocating stench warned us of a dump site ahead. Before us, piles of garbage ascended like skyscrapers.

Each mile, every street corner subjected us to more horrors. My eyes slammed shut like vault doors. I had seen enough..

The next several days I had difficulty eating. As a reporter in war-torn El Salvador I had seen poverty. I had interviewed villagers who had watched their homes decimated by bombs and their crops set ablaze by guerrillas. I was hurt and disillusioned when I returned to the States, yet nothing I had experienced there prepared me for Calcutta.

I felt like an executioner—axe in hand—personally responsible for the plight of so many. Swords of guilt pierced my armor. Why hadn't I done anything to help the starving and diseased? Where was my compassion? I asked myself.

My hotel room became an oasis, a place of refuge from the penetrating heat and the horror that lay in the form of a crippled beggar right outside the hotel entrance.

One evening while at a stop sign, my sense of guilt plunged into depression when a woman, clutching what appeared to be a three-pound infant, reached inside the car window. She grabbed my arm, hoping to find a watch or anything that could be exchanged for food.

As I rolled up the glass, I became angry with myself for shutting the woman out of my life and for feeling so utterly helpless. My questions grew more impatient: "Why, God, does it have to be this way? Why do they have to suffer? And die?" It was only then that I understood why Dr. and Mrs. Buntain were there, persevering when comfort and luxury were only a decision away.

To the credit of India's central government and the government of West Bengal, Calcutta is showing signs of improvement—of again becoming a magnificent city that was once known as the Pearl of the East. Regions of India, such as New Delhi and Madras, are majestic and the people gracious. The Prime Minister's emphasis on education is paramount to the country's resurgence.

Some problems persist, however, despite the government's diligent efforts. Wars, earthquakes, and famines have made Calcutta the land of opportunity for thousands of refugees. Hundreds pour into the city each day, setting up camp on vacant patches of pavement. With an estimated 12 million inhabitants, it's common for a hundred men to jostle in line for one job—a job that may pay five rupees a day (forty U.S. cents).

Even though cows and goats are plentiful, many city-dwellers are undernourished because their religion prevents them from eating meat. Drug addicts and alcoholics wander the streets like the thousands of pye-dogs, with no apparent destination.

The sights and sounds of Calcutta have been widely chronicled, the destitution deeply etched in our minds. Consequently, you will discover that the sequel to *The Compassionate Touch* is much more than an accumulation of stories documenting the tragic realities of Calcutta. This is a diary of hope and God's grace.

You will read true accounts of beggars, orphans, witch doctors, gang leaders, drug addicts, celebrities, and successful businessmen who were confronted with the compassionate words and deeds of a missionary that compelled them to seek a better life. You will read how they were rescued from lives of crime, self-indulgence, sickness, and poverty with the help of one man who dared to obey God.

One chapter, in particular, recounts the stirring story of Kumar. Before I ever met Kumar I dreamed that I, too, was a child straying into the dark alleys of Calcutta, desperately searching for food and a dry place to guard myself from a cruel, unmerciful world. In my dream, I spent the evening under a stack of collapsed cardboard boxes. No blankets, no pillow. As the sun invaded my makeshift hut, I crawled out only to find two large, black-soled shoes waiting for me. A towering white man with dark-rimmed glasses handed me a peanut-butter-and-jelly sandwich. This man with his modest offering and kind words possessed the power of love. His name was Mark Buntain.

For only a few moments, my subconscious experienced the desperate struggle for survival of an Indian child and the subsequent jubilation of knowing Mark Buntain cared. But many of Calcutta's orphans have lived out my dream. They have told me stories of how this peculiar Canadian carried them through his front gate and gave them life, how his loving arms rescued them from death's cradle.

But as my stay in this city concluded and my admiration for the Buntains mounted, it became apparent that *One Man's Compassion* must be more than an idolizing portrait of Mark Buntain. For in Calcutta, I discovered the work of the Calcutta Mission of Mercy is more than one man. It is an outreach comprised of many servants through which Jesus Christ is hugging the world: 22,000 women and children are fed each day; thousands are treated in the Mission's hospital and research center; 6,000 students are enrolled in the Mission's eleven schools; and hundreds more attend the Bible college and vocational schools.

Doug Wead once wrote of Mark Buntain and the work of the Calcutta Mission of Mercy: "It will haunt me for the rest of my life." I can only pray the stories I heard will haunt me as well.

Hal Donaldson

CHAPTER ONE

Kumar

Kumar's cheek rested limply against the mud wall, his legs curled under his seventy-eight-pound frame. He slept that way every night—cramped into a twelve-foot square room with ten others. The feet of his aunt and uncle encompassed him like a picket fence. Once they were asleep, there was no escape. Kumar couldn't even stretch his legs.

Insects frequently scaled his arms, yet he never complained. He knew other children in his bustee* slept on the streets where they were preyed upon by gangs, beggars, and winos. Besides, the cool wall was like a block of ice against his sun scorched face.

His older brother, Shashi, a lanky, hook-nosed teenager, claimed the plot of dirt under a small cot in the far side of the room. But this particular evening Shashi could not sleep. His father had not

* **bustee:** a poor man's village or city slum.

returned home, and that meant there was no money to purchase dinner. Shashi knew his father had either failed to find work that day or had squandered his wages on liquor or prostitutes, as he had so many nights before.

Earlier in the evening, Shashi's mother had wept as she told her children she had no food to feed them.

Shashi was hungry. He wasn't interested in his mother's explanations. His stomach pleaded for just one chapatti,* one handful of rice. No one had ignited his family's chulha* in a day and a half, and flies were feasting on the unused cow dung fuel.

It was well after midnight when Shashi's fears were confirmed. Two mutts barked insults as the slumping silhouette of his father, Birju Mahari, encroached on their territory. Shashi could hear irritated voices and his father's moaning and slurred mumblings.

Shashi rolled over against the wall and closed his eyes, hoping his father would disappear. Suddenly, Mr. Mahari collapsed through the plywood door and fell on top of the boys' uncle. Birju unsteadily picked himself up and staggered to his cot. The clatter woke up the entire family; still no

chapatti: a flat patty made with Indian bread.
chulha: a makeshift stove resembling a campfire.

one dared complain for fear of inciting Birju to a fit of rage.

Shashi's mother, Rekha, remained motionless as her husband fell next to her. She could not help but wonder where, and with whom, Birju had been. Rekha remembered the good life they had once enjoyed. She remembered the respectable position her husband had held before drugs and alcohol transformed him into an unemployable junkie.

For two years, evening after evening, she had watched him sink a needle into his copper skin and release a rope wrapped tightly around his arm like a python. Rekha knew the routine all too well. Moments later, his eyes would close and he would relinquish himself into an artificial nirvana. The memory of it all and the disdain she had for her husband's habits made Rekha want to vomit.

A fly circling above the cot interrupted her nightmarish trance. Birju lay undisturbed. He was snoring unmercifully in Rekha's ear as she contemplated her escape from this dungeon. Hunger pangs gnawed at the children, the landlord demanded money they didn't have, and Birju treated her with increasing disdain and violence.

Rekha knew she had to leave Calcutta—or die. *Tomorrow,* she told herself. Tomorrow she would journey to a place where Birju would never find her. A single tear slid across the bridge of her nose at the thought of leaving her three small children behind. More tears cascaded down her bronze face before dawn.

A Heartbreaking Decision

By mid-morning the following day Birju had departed on his daily pilgrimage to find wages. Like pallbearers, the children promptly gathered their most cherished belongings and toted them down the worn pavement toward their grandmother's hovel. The youngest, Shakira, carried a shiny stone and a rubber ball in a rusted, decorative can.

"Where are you going?" Shakira asked her mother.

"Just away for awhile," Rekha answered nonchalantly, trying to conceal the emotional storm that raged within her.

"Where?" the girl begged, her innocent eyes fixed on her mother's lips.

"Just away to visit some friends," Rekha answered hastily. "Be good to your grandmother. I'll see you again soon."

"Can't we go with you?"

"Can't we go, too?" Kumar asked.

"Why can't we?" pleaded Shashi.

"No, no. You belong here. Just remember how much I love you." The children glued themselves about her waist. "You must go now. Be good," she said, prying them loose from her saree.*

Rekha's throat became hard as one by one the children vanished from her sight. Her cheeks were bathed in tears as she walked away, evading a group of children dancing under the fountain of a water pipe that had burst. She only glanced at a pack of rats nibbling on a dog's carcass a few feet from her path.

Have I done what is right? Will I ever see my babies again? she asked herself.

The rumbling of an overcrowded British double-decker bus suddenly squelched her thoughts. Rekha stopped and whirled around, thinking she should retrieve her children. For a few moments she stood still, searching her mind for an answer.

My future, my destination are unknown. I can't give my children a proper life, she concluded. She turned again and resumed her course, as if guided by fate.

Kumar's Daily Refuge

The children feared their grandmother, who was a scowling hulk of a woman. They scattered in all

saree: an outer garment worn by Indian women that is wrapped around the body and over one shoulder.

directions when her harsh, heavy breathing signaled her approach.

"You are no good!" she snorted. "Your parents would have been better off without you! You're here because no one else wants you."

For Kumar, school was a daily refuge from the wrath of his vexing grandmother. His textbooks were his gods, the classroom his heaven. Kumar enjoyed school and especially looked forward to the daily allotment of rice.

"Thank you," he smiled, hoping the cook would remember him tomorrow and dip the serving spoon deeper into the pot.

Every morning as the school grounds keeper unlocked the gate, he was faithfullly greeted by an ivory-white smile that Kumar flashed through the cast-iron bars. As the youth stood on his tiptoes waiting for the grounds keeper, one could see that the soles of his tattered sandals were disintegrating under his feet.

"Hello, Kumar," the man said. "Stand back so I can open the gate."

As the lad stepped back, dirt streaks from the bars were imprinted on his only set of clothing. His shirt had been resurrected from the local dump site and was two sizes too large. His soiled trousers had been inherited from Shashi. Regardless, Kumar walked through the gate like a child entering Disneyland for the first time. He couldn't help but wonder what it would be like to live at school, inside the gates, sheltered from the worries of endless tomorrows.

After school, the malli* would find the puny, thin-faced boy nestled in a corner of the yard reading a textbook. If Kumar had had his way, he would have stayed on the school grounds forever, at least until old enough to fend for himself. Learning was fun. And being separated from his grandmother made the experience all the more rewarding.

Teachers were amazed by Kumar's rapid progress; he had advanced two grades in nine months and was on the principal's list of excellent students. "If you continue working hard, you will go far," the principal promised Kumar.

Devastated Dreams

On a clear, moonlit night Kumar's scowling grandmother confronted him at the door.

"Why are you so late?" the gray-haired woman snapped.

"I was reading my books," the seven-year-old responded sheepishly.

"What? Didn't I tell you to be home early to help carry water? You're late because of these!"

*malli: a grounds keeper.

She snatched the books from Kumar's arms. "These will stay with me until you get your work done."

"No, grandmother, those are mine." The boy reached out. "They don't belong to you."

Her left eye shifted downward. "I'm paying money for you to go to school. Money I don't have. If you can't help me, then I won't help you. As of now, you are no longer in school."

Kumar began crying as she stomped away. He had no one to appeal to, no place to go. He couldn't join Shashi, who had already returned to their father's hovel, or his sister, Shakira, who was away at boarding school.

Subsequently, Kumar resigned himself to hard, manual labor for meager wages. He spent his waking hours filling receptacles with water for two rupees a day—money that was eventually surrendered to his grandmother. His feet became blistered from carrying man-sized loads on gravel roads. Heavy buckets hung from each end of a wooden rod, forming callouses where it rested on his narrow shoulders. Fourteen hours a day, Kumar carried water.

He hated his grandmother for confiscating his books, for stealing his dreams of an education, for forcing him to do the work of a man. His teeth clenched tighter with every thought of her.

His shoulder was bleeding one evening as he wearily stumbled inside the portal of his grandmother's shoddy house.

"What are you doing?" the woman grunted, her hand draped around a half bottle of illegal liquor.

"I . . . I'm ready to eat," he answered slowly.

"You don't deserve food; you deserve a beating. Since you've come here, nothing has gone right. The gods have cursed me because of you. Leave! Get out! I hate you," she cursed.

The young boy was confused. He despised his grandmother, yet he was afraid to leave. "But where can I go?"

"Leave me, now," she fumed. "I don't care where you go."

"Give me my books first," he bargained. "Give me my books, then I'll go."

She took another swig from the bottle, then stared at the brown elixir. "I used your books to buy me this. Now get out!"

Destitute and Rejected

The little boy launched himself into the darkness. "No one wants me," he muttered as he kicked the side of a crumbling wall. He wandered the streets for hours, dodging policemen and derelicts. Eventually he landed under a banyan tree in a park surrounding Queen Victoria's Palace—a grandiose structure seemingly cut from a mountain of marble.

The next morning he scoured the bazaar for work. Employers laughed in his face. Others angrily pushed him from their doorways. "You're too weak to do me any good. Get out of here," one old man sneered.

Evenings in the park grew cold and lonely. Kumar bundled up in an old, shredded tarpaulin, apparently a remnant from the bed of a military truck. Food was scarce, but the child was too proud to beg. He often scraped worms and ants off the morsels of food he salvaged from garbage heaps. Vomiting contaminated food became a ritual.

The monsoon season was approaching. Floods would follow, creating an above-ground sewage system. Cesspools of excrement and garbage would stagnate above clogged drainage ditches. The streets would become a swamp. Kumar knew he had to find somewhere else to spend his hellish evenings.

A merchant eventually hired Kumar to be his coolie* in exchange for one bowl of rice a day and a hallway to sleep in. Kumar was glad to be under a roof, especially since the nights were darker than

---

* *coolie:* a common laborer hired to carry objects and do other menial tasks.

usual. As the strong monsoon winds buffeted him, Kumar thought about the gods who inhaled and exhaled with great force upon the city.

Kumar hugged the fur of a mangy dog to keep himself warm from the chilled winds. I am so fortunate, he thought as he warmed his nose on the dog's flea-infested ear. But the employer's tolerance of the boy waned as the loads of flour and rice became too heavy for a youth of his stature. Finally, the portly store owner handed the boy a one-rupee note and swept him out into the street.

With nowhere else to go, Kumar returned to the home of his mother and father, who had, at least temporarily, reunited. Rekha embraced her son and kissed his head. Mr. Mahari said nothing. The child was glad to be back in his corner of the tiny room—even if his sprouting legs were more cramped than ever.

A Mysterious White Man

Kumar cringed one evening as he watched his father's veins surface and a needle submerge into his arm with pinpoint accuracy. "Shashi, why does he do that?" he asked.

"I'm not sure."

"Can it kill you?"

"I'm not sure, but I think so," Shashi said, angling his head.

Without warning, the man rose on wobbly legs and reeled outside. The boys stared at one another, wondering where their father was going at this time of night.

By morning, Birju still had not returned home. Two days passed with no word. Then three. No one knew if Rekha's tears reflected sorrow or relief. For a long while the family was uncertain why Birju had left, where he had gone, or if he was even alive.

Then Rekha became ill. For poor families in Calcutta, disease is worse than death because they often must spend their entire lives paying off medical bills. Rekha had no money but desperately needed care.

Rekha's father recalled stories of how a large, mysterious white man with strange powers had fed the poor and helped the sick without asking for money in return. Even witch doctors ask for money, the father thought.

Apprehensively, Rekha's father approached the office of Mark Buntain one splendidly warm afternoon.

"Come on in, and please sit down," Mark greeted, rising from behind a desk overflowing with stacks of paper. "How may I help you?"

The visitor studied the holy man's fine hair and how it was combed straight back. He stared at the furrows of wisdom in his forehead, then fell to one knee in worship of this man, as if Mark were a religious statue.

"Please stand up. There's no need for that," Mark said, tugging on the man's soiled brown jacket.

"My daughter is very sick. Can you give her medicine to make her well?"

"Yes, we have medicine, but we must examine her first," the missionary said. "Will you take me to her?"

"Yes, sahib,"* the small man nodded. "But that isn't necessary. Just give me some medicine for her."

"We must examine her before we can know which medicine is best," Mark insisted.

The old man did not answer.

"The doctors must examine her," Mark repeated.

The old man's eyes flicked from left to right as he pondered the Caucasian's words. He rubbed his nose, then smiled his response.

Overwhelmed

Rekha's father guided Mark through the bustee, a web of huts consisting of mud walls and thatched roofs. Shakira, who had been caring for her mother, grabbed the side of the white man's shirt

sabib: a title given a respectable man.

and hurriedly pulled him into the small shanty. Shashi and Kumar crawled under the cot to make room for the man who would help their mother. Rekha was sitting on the bed, her leg in a full cast, her toes swollen and festered.

"How did this happen?" Mark asked.

"I fell," she answered.

"Is this your only ailment?"

Pulling up her sleeve, the woman unveiled a disease seemingly tattooed on her arm. She knew the missionary recognized the disease, but she told him anyway. "I have leprosy."

Rekha knew that her arm was just the beginning. Someday her fingers and toes would be stumps and her nose nothing more than an oozing aperture of warm pus.

Mark knew leprosy's bane all too well. He had spent entire days in leper colonies suppressing his own fears and smiling into disfigured faces. The preacher was seldom at a loss for words, but he was beginning to feel overwhelmed.

Mark was tired, Sunday's sermons were unprepared, and the stack of requests for assistance equalled the listings in a metropolitan phone book. He had spent the entire morning counseling and praying with a drug addict. The previous day included visits to a woman whose baby had tuberculosis and a man whose wife was committing adultery.

"Where is your husband?" he said after a long silence.

"He left when he found out I had leprosy."

"Dear woman," Mark offered, "will you allow me to pray for you?" He could see she was frightened. "Please, you'll be all right. I'm here to help you."

"Yes," she whispered. "Pray."

Four cat-like eyes shined from the patch of darkness under the cot. A white man had never been in this room before. The boys weren't sure what he could do; they were just glad he was there.

"Dear God, be with this woman. Show her You love her and her family. Touch her body," Mark prayed in a weary, raspy voice. A few moments later, he stood, ducking his head to keep from puncturing the straw ceiling. "I want her to come to our hospital. Is that okay?"

The grandfather hesitated and looked down. "We have no money."

"Don't worry about that. We want to make her well. It won't cost you any money."

"No money?" he asked.

"No money."

The old man bowed his head to the missionary as his eyes began to water. "Thank you, sahib, thank you."

"Thank God, my dear man. By the way, bring the two boys to my office tomorrow." The boys' heads popped from under the mattress like turtles from their shells. "Yes, you two," Mark smiled. He would make sure they were cared for, too. Eventually Shashi would be admitted to a youth shelter and Kumar would be enrolled in Mark's school.

A Place for Kumar

Once again, Kumar proved to be a bright and willing student. Thus, his teachers expressed concern when the child began showing visible signs of neglect. Not only did he fall asleep in class, but his clothes were filthy and he was coughing from deep within. Then one morning, Mark discovered the boy curled up with his dog on the street outside the school's front gate.

"Kumar!" Mark exclaimed, shaking the boy's shoulder. "What are you doing here so early?"

Kumar was half-conscious. "I, uh," he stuttered, "was waiting to talk to you, Uncle."

"Listen, son," Mark said in a serious tone. "Tell me the truth. You slept here last night, didn't you?"

"Yes, Uncle. My mother is too sick to worry about me. It's better if I'm not there," he said, rubbing the sleep from his eyes.

"Come in, son." The missionary turned the key and motioned for the dog to wait outside. "We'll find a place for you to stay, Kumar. I'll send you to my wife. She'll find a place. She always does."

Begrudgingly, Kumar thought, They'll send me to a place where I'm not wanted, somewhere they won't have to worry about me.

Huldah Buntain stared warmly at the walnut-skinned waif for a few moments. "How old are you, Kumar?" she smiled. Her light red hair glistened under the light fixture, and her brown eyes beamed at him intently.

"Ten," he answered sharply.

"Ten? A big boy like you must be at least fifteen," she teased.

"I'm ten."

"Ten's a good age," Huldah said, jotting a note on the pad in front of her. "I understand your brother is in our youth shelter program."

Kumar nodded.

"The first thing we're going to do is get you a bath, some clean clothes, and some good food. How's that sound?"

Kumar sat up in his chair, his eyes so wide open they hurt.

"You may live here on the church grounds awhile, but you'll have a few chores to do to earn your keep," she said.

Why would they be so kind to me? Kumar asked himself. But for the moment he didn't care. He was just grateful to have a blanket and a full stomach.

The next morning, after her car purred to a halt in the church parking lot, Huldah was greeted by a handsome, well-dressed boy. "Hello, ma'am. May I carry your suitcase for you?" Kumar asked, grinning.

"Sure," she chuckled as she handed him the briefcase, "but call me Auntie."

"Yes, Auntie," he grinned, marveling at the brilliant colors of her cotton skirt and the glinting beads that dangled from her neck.

Unconditional Love

The sun was sinking behind the church that afternoon when Huldah noticed Kumar leaning against a post, reading. She fastened her narrow fingers onto his head and steered him into her car.

"Let's go for a ride," she suggested.

The boy could not remember the last time he had ridden in an automobile. He stuck his head outside the window to let the wind slap against his face and laughed as it combed his hair backwards.

"Be careful," she warned as an oncoming bus sped by, twelve inches from his door.

Huldah led the child through a gate and up the bright red steps to their flat. By Western standards, the Buntain's apartment was meager. To Kumar, it was the Taj Mahal.

As she served him a plate of chicken casserole and vegetables, Kumar was again bewildered by her kindness. Why is she doing this? What do they want in return? A myriad of questions danced in his mind, suspicion imprinted on his dark, sunken eyes.

Finally he asked her, "Why are you nice to me?"

"Because I like you," she replied.

"Why?"

"I guess because God has given you to us as a friend. And when God gives you something, you do your best to take care of it. God loves you, Kumar. And so do we."

For months afterwards, Kumar pondered what "Auntie Huldah" had said about God's love. From his second floor window he watched the Buntains carry squalid children with bloated stomachs into the compound.

"Why are they so kind and why do they work so hard for people they don't even know?" he asked himself. "They even sent my mother to a special clinic and fed my family. Why do they do all these things?" He could find no answers.

Mr. Pearly's Gates

The ceiling fans were whipping furiously one June Sunday as the congregation sang its usual repertoire of choruses. "Jesus, Jesus, Jesus, I've got

Him on my mind'' could be heard throughout the neighborhood. Pastor Buntain stepped to the pulpit. Raindrops drummed against the large, rectangular windows, casting soft echoes throughout the sanctuary. Kumar drove his hands into his pockets and slumped into his chair as the rain slid down the beveled glass. He fixed his eyes on the white man who had rescued him from poverty and certain death, the man who had shown him the meaning of love.

"Many of you," Mark began waving his hand, "come here every Sunday, but you do not have a relationship with Jesus Christ. And, consequently, one day Jesus will not welcome you through the pearly gates."

Kumar conjured up an image of Jesus as the durwan* refusing to let him pass through the cast-iron gate into the schoolyard. "Today," Mark continued, "Jesus wants to adopt you into His family. He wants to be your heavenly Father. He wants you to enter heaven's gates to live forever."

Moisture began to accumulate in Kumar's eyes. Mark said, "This morning, if you want to be a child of God, come down here and kneel before Him." Kumar was the first to jump to his feet. Huldah was just a few strides behind him, anxious to help lead the boy to Christ.

---

* *durwan:* a gatekeeper.

"Auntie Huldah," Kumar glanced up from the altar, "will Jesus let me inside Mr. Pearly's gates?"

Huldah was laughing beneath her tears. "Kumar, you don't mean Mr. Pearly's gates; you mean the pearly gates."

Kumar nodded.

"Yes," Huldah said, hugging the boy's shoulder, "Jesus will let you live with Him forever."

Kumar looked away for a moment, then closed his eyes.

"Jesus," he prayed, "thank You for letting me enter Your gates. I want to live with You someday. But if it's all right, I want to stay with Uncle Mark and Auntie a little while longer."

Huldah could not help herself. She sat on the altar and laughed and cried.

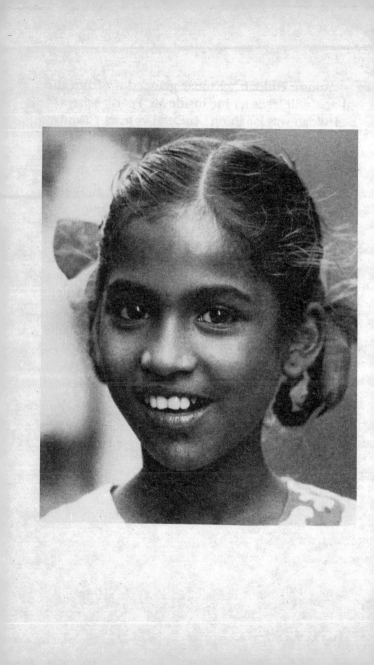

CHAPTER TWO

Shukla

The room was black, except for a sliver of light splashing under the door. Suddenly, a single candle ignited. Its reddish flame looked like a fiery ball in the middle of the room, and a half lit face hovered eerily above the candle. Blackness obscured the left side of the woman's face. She turned her back to the candle and knelt, her spine parallel to the floor.

A human-sized statue was now visible. Smaller statues lined the shelves. The bedroom resembled a museum, except it was cold and dark. The light reflected against the statue's glossy exterior, the contoured edges of the clay image barely traceable. Its charcoal finish was eclipsed by its dangling, bright red tongue. A snake and skull necklace flowed between its breasts. Flowers smelling like blood decorated the base of the statue, inches from where the woman's face was to the ground.

"Hear my request, oh mighty goddess," Gita prayed. "My daughter, Shukla, is crippled. She is not like other children. Please take away this evil curse that binds her. She is yours if you will make her well. Great goddess, I believe you have the power to make her well," the woman sobbed.

Suddenly, the door to her bedroom-sanctuary swung open. The holy ritual had been desecrated. "The gods will be angry," the woman moaned. "They have been offended!" She then hastened to expel the intruder.

"Mother, what are you doing?" her daughter interrogated. "*Why* are you doing this?"

"Shukla, shut the door," the terrified woman commanded, hoping to return to her prone position and pacify the gods.

Shukla obeyed.

Thirty minutes later, Gita emerged from her cave. "For *you*," she hissed at her crippled daughter. "That's why I pray to the gods. You will never walk again until you stop angering the gods. The white man's god is a false god. He does not exist."

"He does, Mother; you know it. You promised God you would follow Him if I got better. How can you forget?"

"He has done nothing," Gita rebuked.

"He has. Look, I can walk without my braces." The twelve-year-old pointed to her legs.

"A powerful god would heal completely, not partially," the mother persisted. "If you get well, Shukla, it's because of my prayers to the goddess!"

The young girl ground her teeth together, shaking her head from side to side, frustration gnawing at her stomach.

Shukla's deep dimples were so captivating they minimized the imperfection of a crossed right eye. The girl's tight skin and high cheekbones were sometimes veiled by her long, sweeping midnight hair. One, however, could not easily disregard her inert right foot, which slid along the ground behind her. Still, for the first time in her life, Shukla was proud. No longer did she don the braces that pronounced to the world her inferiority. She was getting well. She was certain of it.

Stricken With Polio

Shortly after Shukla's birth, Gita and her husband had knelt before their clay images, thanking the spirits for giving them a healthy child. Shukla was Gita's trophy, a sign that she had found favor with the gods. Other newborns conceived in the bustee had been afflicted with deformities and disease—a sure sign that the gods were displeased. Gita carried her prize everywhere: the market, the temple, the pavement spigot.

Ominous, layered clouds converged one afternoon, forcing Gita to postpone her journey to the market. She would stay home with her baby today, and because piercing winds knifed through the gaping planks of her shack, Gita kept a blanket on Shukla at all times.

Gita was scrubbing her husband's other pair of pants in a small, corroded pot when she heard her baby coughing. The struggling sounds beckoned Gita to her child's side. Shukla's face was warm, and she had emptied her bowels all over the blanket.

Surely, it's nothing more than a minor infection, the young mother thought.

An hour passed, and the baby continued to whimper and cough. Her face appeared swollen, her eyes lifeless.

Gita frantically snatched a pouch that contained the family's life savings. She clutched the rupees tightly in her hand as if they were a panacea. Holding her daughter close to her breast, the distraught mother bounded through a pile of decaying trash into the street. She freed one arm to summon a passing rickshaw.*

"My baby is sick," she screamed. "Hurry! To the nearest hospital!"

An elderly man pulled the two-wheeled, wooden-spoked carriage with surprising strength. His bare feet were like horse hooves, undaunted

---

* *rickshaw:* a wooden-spoked carriage with two large wheels and two protruding rods used to pull the unmotorized taxi.

by the sharp stones and toxic puddles. His graying beard faded into his sun bleached shirt. Gita did not need to implore him to run faster. His bulging calf muscles surged through a sea of honking vehicles without hesitation.

Gita cradled her sick child in her arms, oblivious to the bumpy roads. She felt like a thousand eyes were focused on her chariot, as if they were privy to a sin she had committed—a sin deserved of such punishment. She could sense the gods glaring at her from the heavens. "Please," she begged, "let my girl live."

A line of patients suffering from gastritis, tuberculosis, and other illnesses stretched outside the hospital entrance. Gita panicked. "I can't wait," she yelled into the crowd. "My baby is dying! I must get through."

"You're not the only one here," corrected a wry old woman, her hairy chin bobbing rapidly.

No one moved aside. More people came and went. Gita could feel the heat of her baby's body intensify.

Then, almost like a matinee super hero, a white-coated doctor rescued the mother and her child from the hive of patients. He placed the baby on a table covered with a dingy white sheet, saying little as he examined the child. Perspiration crawled down his sideburns. "Your daughter," he finally said, "has a severe case of typhoid fever."

The mother burrowed her ringed fingers into the table. The crumpled skin under her eyes swelled. Tears burst from her eyes. Guiding her to a chair, the doctor noticed the woman's money pouch trapped between her quivering hands. "For fifty rupees I'll help your daughter."

Gita dumped the contents of the pouch into her lap. "I have only thirty," she sobbed.

"That will do for now. But you must pay more later."

In the coming months, the mother learned more distressing news: Shukla had been stricken with polio, leaving her legs limp and useless.

Desperate for Answers

Gita and her husband slaved in prayer before the gods. Their last rupee was given to the priest to offer a puja* in behalf of Shukla. Yet by age three the child showed no signs of improvement. The parents concluded that the gods had deserted them.

"What have we done to be sentenced to such torture? What must we do to be pardoned by the gods?" they asked. Every ritual was tried, every

* *puja:* a ceremonial worship consisting of an offering, prayer, chants, mantras, and other displays of praise to the Hindu gods.

prayer offered. Still the girl suffered. Gita grew discouraged and angry while her husband suppressed his bitterness with alcohol.

"Take her to Mark Buntain's church," a neighbor beckoned one day. "Jesus is there. He will heal your daughter."

"Jesus?" Gita asked, wondering if He were some powerful priest or god who had escaped her. "Is He a god?"

"He is the only God. Bring Shukla with you tonight and meet Him."

Gita believed in many gods, not one almighty spirit. Such foolishness, in fact, infuriated her. But this neighbor who had introduced her to Jesus was one of her finest customers, often purchasing her homemade pickles.

Reluctantly, she situated herself in the back row of the sanctuary one brisk evening. Desperation and obligation had ushered her there, and now this God would have to perform a miracle for her to believe in Him. Just in case, she held the baby upright so this God could not claim He had not seen her feeble child.

"Is that Jesus?" Gita asked as she pointed at a tall white man on the stage.

The neighbor smirked, leaning over to explain. "No, that is a priest of Jesus. His name is Pastor Buntain. Jesus is already here. His Spirit is here."

"Well, when will He heal my baby?"

"I don't know, maybe not tonight."

"You mean I must return to this place again?"

The neighbor nodded.

Gita did not resist displaying her disappointment at her neighbor's response.

She labored down the steps seconds after the benediction. Her neighbor trailed closely at her right side. The young mother's eyes sank with each step, warding off potential greeters. "This so-called God has no power," she grumbled to herself.

Suddenly, a deep voice parted the crowd. "Wait!" Gita took three more steps before Mark's hand harnessed her shoulder. "Hello, my dear woman. I'm Pastor Buntain. May I ask your name?"

"Gita," she responded nervously.

"And hers?" he motioned to the infant in her arms.

"Shukla."

"Hello, Shukla." Mark dabbed her nose with his index finger.

"Ma'am, what is your daughter's ailment?"

"Polio," she answered, wondering if he was going to attempt to heal her right there.

"This girl will be all right," the white man assured. "Bring her to our hospital tomorrow. God bless you."

Gita walked away astonished by the priest's confidence. She wondered if the white man had noticed that the child's legs were so withered her feet faced opposite directions.

"How can this man know Shukla will be all right?" she asked her neighbor.

"He talks to God. He is a holy man."

Please Heal My Daughter

Doctors eventually performed corrective surgery on Shukla's legs; the girl was still under anesthesia when her mother entered the recovery room. Gita stepped quietly to her sleeping daughter's side as nurses adjusted beds nearby.

"God, I do not know You, but if You are real, please heal my daughter." Gita sat on the end of the bed, her chin bowed. "I'll dedicate this girl to You if You make her well."

Mark was standing in the doorway when the woman opened her eyes. His frame prevented the hall light from intruding the already dim room. "He heard you," Mark assured.

"I hope so," she droned.

"Oh, He has."

"Thank you for helping my daughter," Gita praised.

"Please, just be grateful to God."

Several days later, the child left the hospital in bulky braces up to her waist. Orthopedic surgeons recommended shoes with special soles to help her bones grow properly. One shoe was two inches higher than the other. At first, it was awkward for Shukla, but before long she grew accustomed to the cumbersome shackles about her legs and feet.

Nevertheless, after four years of therapy, braces, prayers, and visits from Mark Buntain, Shukla's legs were as gnarled and inoperable as ever.

Gita decided her praise for Mark Buntain and his God had been premature. Furthermore, she resolved that Shukla would never overcome her unsightly limp, though she could never muster the courage to confess her fleeting faith to her daughter.

Like a sentinel, Shukla stationed herself outside her shelter to watch other children run and jump in the street. Their legs had such vitality and grace. "Someday I'll run," she promised herself. "Mama said so."

The children gathered in a loose huddle to select teams for a game of soccer. Some were admiring the smooth basketball-turned-soccer ball when one of the boys shouted, "Your team gets Shukla." The children laughed. Shukla's attempt to restrain the tears failed. Her brother then scooped her up on his back and gave her a ride inside.

"Why do they make fun of me, Mama?" she cried, her cheeks streaked with tears.

"They're just having fun. They don't mean to hurt you."

"Why can't I be like other kids?"

"You will, Shukla. Someday you will." Gita turned her head to cloak her own tears of disbelief.

Which God Heals?

Shukla was nearly nine when it became apparent another operation would be necessary.

The sweltering heat of Calcutta pushed the thermometer to 108 degrees; the sun's intense rays were punishing the entire city, including Shukla's hospital room. While other patients laid on top of their sheets, Shukla buried her unsightly legs beneath her linens. The child's frail body hardly created a lump in the bed as Pastor Buntain surveyed the room that resembled a MASH ward during the Korean War.

"Aren't you warm, Shukla?" he inquired.

"I'm fine," she smiled.

"Well, the doctors tell me the same. You're going to be fine. You're going to walk soon because God wants you to walk."

Shukla grinned from ear to ear at the big, kind man. How she wanted to believe in him and his God.

"Mama," Shukla asked when she arrived home from the hospital following her second surgery, "who is God?"

"There are many gods, which one?"

The girl glanced up, ignoring her mother's question. "Then *who* created the gods? Do they have a father?"

"No, not really. They're just all gods."

"Which god is Mr. Buntain's God? He said his God is going to make me well."

Gita bent down and scowled into her daughter's searching eyes. "There is no such god. Our gods will heal you. Not the white man's God. Do you understand me?" she shouted.

Shukla was startled. "Yes, Mama," she said, though thinking it unfair of her mother to treat this God with such disrespect.

The young girl lay awake at night thinking how good this God must be to care about her legs. "He must be kind and powerful to make people well. Is He anything like Mr. Buntain?" she wondered. "He must be for Pastor Buntain to worship Him."

A year later, Shukla was able to wear regular shoes and shed her braces. "See, Mama, God is making me well," she rejoiced.

Gita was unsure which god Shukla meant, but nodded her head in approval in the presence of the attending physician from Mark's hospital.

Drawn to the Living God

Later, annoyed by her daughter's inquisitiveness, Gita forbade Shukla to talk about the white man's

God or to attend the Christian church. On Sunday mornings, the girl watched from her door as some neighbors strolled to churches. Women wearing clinking metal anklets and their finest veiled sarees paraded by. The men in dress shirts, ties, and cotton tunics sported hairstyles groomed with precious ointments. Shukla longed to follow them, but she feared her mother would disown her if she did.

With each passing Sunday, her desire to discover more about the Christian God intensified. "If only Mama would understand and not punish me for going to His church," she dreamed.

One torrid summer afternoon the twelve-year-old sneaked out to find this God she loved, to pay Him homage for fortifying her legs. Although she limped awkwardly toward the sanctuary, she was no longer prisoner to her braces. For that she was grateful. The tall church building sent arctic chills down Shukla's back, so much so that she was frozen in her path momentarily.

"This is it. This is where Mr. Buntain's God is." Shukla climbed the church steps, which she viewed as a path to God's emerald throne. From her seat, the young girl inspected the sanctuary, trying but failing to locate the statue of this God. "It must be beautiful," she thought; "something deserving of a loving God."

Mark began reading from a book called Romans: "All have sinned and fall short of the glory of God" (Romans 3:23). He continued with another passage: "The wages of sin is death, but the gift of God is eternal life" (Romans 6:23).

Shukla understood the meaning of eternal life. Her mother had taught her the principles of reincarnation. But this man spoke of living in heaven—a place foreign to her. She didn't know its location. She just knew she wanted to be there if that was where her Healer lived. That day Shukla went forward to have Mark pray for her so she could receive Christ as her personal Savior.

Mark smiled as he asked the young girl to kneel at the altar. Shukla did not feel any strange sensations or hear any mysterious voices as Mark prayed. Rather, all at once, she was relieved, happy, and feeling loved like she never had before.

Leaving the sanctuary—feeling like a new person—she experienced a twinge of fear. She asked herself, "How will I explain this to Mama?"

Answered Prayer

Years passed and Shukla was a young, independent woman. She was continuing to gain strength in her legs when misfortune again beset the family. Her father had lost his job and was drinking heavily, and her older brother had run away.

"Mama, don't cry," Shukla comforted. "Nothing is impossible with God. I will fast and pray, and the God who is healing me will give Father a new job and bring my brother home. Then you will know the real God."

Gita turned from her daughter and crept back into her cubicle to perform holy rites before the gods. Shukla fell to her knees outside her mother's den and began praying.

"Dear God, please forgive my mother for her unbelief. She is a good woman. Please show her that her images are evil; that You are the only God. Show her how powerful and loving You are by bringing my brother home and giving Father a new job. Please, God, hear my request."

Shukla's younger brother ridiculed her prayer, saying, "Shukla, you are a fool to believe this God can help you. Even if there was such a god, why do you think He would listen to you anyway?"

With that, he then proceeded to pour water over her head. Barely faltering, she resumed her mission. Her feeble knees rested in a puddle on the clay floor. Drops fell from her soggy mop of hair and dripped onto her closed eyes. The attacks persisted as her tormentor threw objects and made disturbing noises. Shukla's knees sank deeper. Yet she never retaliated. Her God's Bible taught differently.

To the amazement of everyone, within a week God had answered Shukla's prayers. Her brother returned to his family, and a new job became available for her father.

As Shukla knelt in her room to give thanks to her God, the plywood door suddenly opened. She girded herself, half-expecting to be ambushed with a pail of water. Instead someone knelt beside her.

"Please tell your God I am grateful," a familiar voice uttered. "I now know He is real."

Shukla shrouded her mother with her affectionate arms. As the two embraced without a word, Shukla smiled to the ceiling. She knew the ceremonial incense candles in her mother's cubicle had flickered for the last time.

"You tell him, Mama. He wants to be your God, too," Shukla cheered.

CHAPTER THREE

Raj

"Young men, give me your attention, please," the Irish Brother said, clearing his throat. Immediately two thousand boys stood at attention, their eyes riveted on the rotund school director. Not even a sniffle could be heard.

"Today you will witness the punishment of one of your fellow students," the religious man announced, his wrinkled and brown spotted hands steadying the microphone. His balding head protruded from his gown like a toe through a worn brown sock. "He was caught smoking in the lavatory. Consequently, he will receive thirty-five slashes. Raj, please come forward."

Students clenched their teeth to keep from laughing while the ten-year-old strode defiantly toward the director. With each step, the chant to plead for mercy or run for the nearest exit beat louder in Raj's ears. But my friends in the Scorpion gang will think I'm a coward, he reasoned. Finally, he stepped onto the two-foot riser where

Brother McConnell was standing. A chair had been placed in the center of the platform. Raj knew why it was there.

"Lower your pants, Raj," the director ordered. Sixty seconds later the boy was in position for the "execution." His pants encircled his ankles as he bent over the chair. His buttocks were facing the audience when the greased bamboo stick smacked against raw flesh.

Some of the boys were smiling; others flinched with every collision. By the tenth slash, red lines etched his pastel-shaded rear end. Again he considered pleading for the Brother's mercy, but he knew his fellow gang members would disapprove of any visible reaction to the beating. He remembered one of his father's favorite sayings, "Only those who are weak cry." Thus, Raj tucked his lips inside his mouth to keep from whimpering and saying something he would later regret.

Joining the Scorpions

Raj's father, a commanding officer who had served in World War II, ruled his home as he had his regiment. With military strictness he enforced a dress code and assigned duties to his young charges. Desertion from one's responsibilities resulted in a confrontation with a leather army belt.

Even though Raj disliked his father's discipline, he dreamed of being just like him: rough and sturdy. Raj had inherited his father's shaggy eyebrows, slender cheeks, and pointed chin. His tapered haircut was strictly military.

Raj's parents were proud. Their son was attending one of the finest boarding schools in India. It was there, however, that Raj became a "Scorpion."

Raj witnessed an example of the gang's coercive skills and ruthless influence his first day at the esteemed school. He was gulping tea and toast in the dining facility when in stampeded five boys. The room grew silent as they strutted by each table.

"Who are they?" Raj whispered to the Anglo-Indian beside him.

"Those are the Scorpions. Be quiet!" the boy ordered as the band approached their table. He then stared nervously at his plate, his eyes too large to be pondering his food. He continued staring to avoid eye contact with the gang leader, a tall, angular boy.

The gang began peeling kids off the opposite end of the table. Raj merely chuckled. The leader's long arms were confiscating slices of toast from those nearby. His sneers made the younger boys tremble. His eyes blazed like fire—beautiful but terrifying. Another gang member across from Raj wore his black hair pulled back behind his ears, a single strand bisecting his forehead.

"Do they steal food often?" Raj asked the fearful boy.

"Yes, they get whatever they want," he answered. Color returned to his face as the gang rose to leave.

Raj remained unruffled by the Scorpions' displays of power, finding humor in their exploits. After all, Raj was one who preferred *issuing* orders to *taking* them.

Within several weeks he had become a feared member of the gang. And thereafter, receiving slashes in class was a weekly routine.

Devilish Defiance

One afternoon the "a la carte" van was left unlocked. The Scorpions pilfered it like ants attacking a picnic.

"Do you know where the food is?" Brother Wilson asked, marching into Raj's room shortly after the heist.

"No," Raj replied. "Why ask me? There are a thousand others who could have taken it."

"I'm aware of that. I'm not necessarily accusing you. But we both know you and your friends are in the middle of most of the trouble around here."

Raj, with his T-shirt sleeves rolled up to his armpits, stared defiantly. "I said it's not here."

"Okay," the priest conceded. "If I find it elsewhere, I'll owe you an apology. But if you're involved, I'm sending you home."

"Well, then, I guess I'll await your apology—sir," Raj insisted, his jaw thrust upward.

The frustrated instructor slammed the door behind him as he left the room. Raj, with a devilish smile, then extracted a piece of the missing cheese from beneath his mattress.

His grades alone were grounds for expulsion. Raj refused to study or do his homework, choosing to experience school as he would an amusement park. Whippings, restrictions, public humiliations—nothing could motivate the boy to learn. He preferred mischief.

One afternoon, Brother McConnell called Raj and a classmate named Shyamal into his office. The boys had been caught fighting on the school grounds, and now they awaited the director, who would soon mete out their punishment.

"If you dare tell him about me selling you cigarettes, the Scorpions will pay you back," Raj threatened.

"I won't tell if you give me another pack," Shyamal whispered angrily.

Just then the principal entered the room like a judge about to entertain testimony. He surprised them both, however, by not asking for details of the fight. The greased bamboo cane materialized, leaving little to be said.

The two boys had difficulty sitting the next few days and a harder time settling their differences. When Raj bloodied Shyamal's nose in another playground bout, again Father McConnell's stick appeared. Only this time Raj was pegged as the lone culprit. Shyamal gleefully exited the principal's office and lofted a sinister-looking grin in Raj's direction.

Raj's sneering facial response was his way of saying, "Shyamal, you're going to pay for this."

Moments later, Raj's shrill screams echoed the snapping sounds of the bamboo rod. But because the howls grew louder with each swat, the principal decided to reduce the prescribed number of blows. Raj silently congratulated himself on a most convincing performance.

Midnight Escapades

At seven-thirty one December evening, a large bell over the school's entrance signaled the students to go to their rooms for a study period. For the Scorpions, however, it was a signal to prepare for another unauthorized excursion into town. They hopped over the six-foot cement wall by laddering up a barrel.

After hijacking a carrier tricycle and smoking some bidis,* the boys loitered outside an all-night theater. One of them, while trying to sneak inside, was apprehended by the theater manager. The obese, white-coated man changed his mind about calling the authorities after the gang members surrounded him, their hands closing into fists.

The following morning, the Scorpions returned to school through the front gate like a goose-stepping squadron. One by one they were escorted into the principal's office to receive their floggings. The hallway echoed with screams, yelps, and grunts.

Raj, too, had expected a lashing when he entered the office, but he was mistaken.

"You are not going to receive any slashes," the Brother calmly told him. "Your parents have sent word that you must return to Calcutta. Evidently, they are no longer able to afford our fees. I'm sorry. They'll be placing you in another school. If you were a finer student, a finer citizen, we might be able to help you. But the truth is, you have not done your best, and you have been disruptive."

No disputing words came to Raj's lips. He stared at the wall.

* *bidis:* a poor man's cigarette.

Listening from the bench in the hallway, Raj's comrades were baffled by the silence.

"You are to leave tomorrow morning. Brother Wilson will take you." McConnell strolled to the front of his desk and sat on the corner. For the first time, Raj noticed that the Brother wore white socks under his floor-length cloak.

"Raj, I want you to listen to some advice. Don't think you can get what you want just because you're tough. There are a lot tougher people out there. You're still young. If you start studying now, you'll be able to do something with your life, something more than hurting other people." Brother McConnell paused, then offered his hand. "I hope you do well, Raj."

Raj looked at the extended pale palm, then walked out without acknowledging the hand that had inflicted so much pain.

Back to Calcutta

Calcutta seemed like an endless montage of windows and signs as Raj and his chaperone rode past a market he had visited as a child. He had forgotten the throngs of wild pye-dogs that prowled the streets. Even the aroma of stagnant sewage and the memory of beggars blocking the sidewalks had escaped him. In comparison, Brother McConnell's school was Eden, and suddenly Raj regretted more than ever that he had to leave.

Although enrollment in his new school in Calcutta required less of the family's resources, Raj began spending more and more family money on cigarettes and alcohol. And when there were no rupees to take from home, he resorted to thievery to support his habits. An open door or an unattended sidewalk store were easy prey for the boy's fast hands.

Raj soon joined a local gang that was headquartered on the roof of the leader's home. Manaj's family worked for a major corporation, so the leader's right jean pocket was always stuffed with a roll of bills. His house even had a porcelain toilet.

Manaj's six-foot muscular build bulged from beneath his tight shirt and European jeans. His large hands freely distributed bottles of liquor nearly every night. The flatness of his face gave him an eerie look, as if he had no eye sockets. Violence was engraved on his face in the form of two scars on his right cheek.

His ragtag platoon proudly sported the trademarks of a street gang: headbands, earrings, scraggly locks of hair, cigarettes bent from lips like straws, knives concealed under T-shirts, and blazing eyes that feasted on hatred's venom.

Hashish smoke frequently formed a cloud over the terrace of their meeting place, obscuring the luminous moon. Alcohol and stronger drugs often cast a spell over the young men. They would wake at daybreak slobbering onto the tile floor. Sometimes they roamed the streets after dark looking for a fight to pick, a store to rob, or a prostitute to harass.

Confrontation at Home

Raj had tried desperately to conceal his alcohol use and criminal activities from his family. He had, consequently, not expected a confrontation when he slipped into his house late one night, following a typical evening with the gang. But there on a stool just inside the door awaited his father.

"Where have you been?" his father asked, his voice firm.

"With friends, sir."

"I know, but what have you been doing with your friends?"

Raj hesitated. "Just studying . . . talking." He looked away to keep his father from smelling his breath.

His father was not to be fooled. "It smells like you've been drinking. Have you?"

"Yes, sir, I have." Raj's voice was confident, but he could see his father wince at his answer.

"Do you know that you are forbidden to drink?"

"Yes."

Someone began to stir in the next room. The man's voice heightened. "You have deliberately disobeyed my orders," he said as if an unpardonable sin had been committed.

"I know," Raj admitted.

"You have disgraced your mother and your family name," the father continued. The rest was buried deep in his throat. He clearly wanted to say more but instead he threw up his hands in frustration. "We'll talk tomorrow!"

The follow-up conversation, however, never took place. As a military officer, his father acknowledged the breakdown in communication as a personal failure to control his ranks. Guilt and disappointment created an even deeper chasm between him and his son. They stopped talking altogether, like two mutes separated by an impenetrable wall.

Gang Wars

A rival gang ruled an area of real estate three streets to the north of Manaj's house. Past battles had left permanent scars and injuries, including a deep gash above one gang member's eye from an unexpected knife. For years the two gangs had fought, each with a history of victories and setbacks. But the confrontations were escalating. Their arsenals now included homemade smoke bombs and several small handguns.

The streets were empty one evening. Even the dogs had vanished. As advertised, the gangs were preparing for war—a war that would determine supremacy in the community. Ultimately the victor would win nothing more than respect, but for the gang members that was a worthy prize. By the following morning, the entire neighborhood would know the outcome.

"Remember, we'll be outnumbered," Manaj warned, almost as if he welcomed the odds. "So we must hit them hard and fast. Choose a man, inflict some pain, then find another. Let's go!"

Drugs and alcohol awaited the gang's return—for what they hoped would be a victory celebration. The gladiators toted steel pipes, boards, and blades down the stairs behind their commander. They cautiously approached the yard of a vacant building where the gang leaders had scheduled this battle.

The rival warriors huddled together like a pack of wild boars awaiting the word from their leader. The young commander rolled up his sleeves. His bangs completely covered his temples. He clutched a sword-like scrap of metal in his hand. The two factions faced one another, two boxers trying to intimidate the other with their seething eyes.

"Manaj, we weren't sure you were coming," the opponent shouted across the war zone.

"We're here, Biju," Manaj asserted. "I see you brought your little sisters," he smirked, baiting the adversary he knew so well.

"You'll regret what you say!" the boy spouted.

"I don't think so," Manaj countered, waving his fist at the rival group. "It looks like you brought some extra bodies. What's the matter, you think you need an advantage?"

Watching the encounter, Raj realized for the first time that Manaj was not as fearless as his threats. He, too, wanted to even the odds.

Biju ran his finger down the blunt edge of his sword, then motioned for a few boys to step out of the fight. "Enough of you. Now!" he charged.

The squads converged on one another in a sudden frenzy. Raj drove his head into another boy's chest and staked his back to the earth. Weapons scattered. The boy rolled Raj beside him with a vicious tug on his hair, prompting a trickle of blood to flow into his brow. The broad shouldered warrior pinned Raj to the ground with a kick to the side. Then another kick. Finally, Raj scrambled to his feet, his diaphragm bruised with invisible footprints.

"Come on," the boy taunted. Raj re-armed himself with his hand-hewn club. His opponent had only his bare fists. Raj connected with his opponent's thigh, then, with one swoop wedged the board between the boy's ribs. Like a conquering soldier, Raj basked above his spoilage.

To his gang, Raj was a hero, but the accolades did little to combat his fear that his parents would hear of his part in the battle. Raj prayed to the gods that his parents would never learn of their son's crimes and many wicked activities.

Making the Break

Several months passed. It was a warm evening, and Manaj had stared at his buddies long enough. Everything was too quiet, too uneventful. His booze was tasteless. He studied his bidi and threw it beneath his sole.

"Let's go find us a young girl and have some fun," he said. The suggestion was met with eager eyes.

"What do you want to do with the girl?" Raj asked in a perplexed tone.

Manaj grinned. "You know, give her a thrill."

"You mean rape her?" Raj's eyebrows arched.

"Maybe," Manaj said. "What's wrong with you?"

"I'm not going to ruin some girl. Let's just pay one and . . ."

"We don't need to pay for it," Manaj sneered. The gang members were astonished by Raj's resistance. He had instigated many of their most daring assaults, and now he was shying away from a relatively easy task.

"Listen, Raj, either you're with us or you're not," Manaj sneered.

"Then I'm not." There was a hush as Raj started to retreat down the stairwell. His rapid footsteps sounded like a tribal drum. The beating stopped. "Manaj," he shouted back. Only Raj's head was now visible as Manaj spun around.

"What?"

"Be careful. If you don't watch out, you're not going to live long."

Raj didn't wait for a response.

Divine Appointments

Raj worked as an errand boy, waiter, and sales representative before a friend landed him a better job. With more money in his pockets, Raj sank deeper into alcohol and drugs. The pectoral muscles he had built by diligently hoisting barbells turned to pudding. The veins in the yellow of his eyes grew repulsively distinct. His cheeks became drawn, his beard scraggly.

While standing in line to see a movie one afternoon, Raj wiped the nape of his neck and ignored the pleas of a blind beggar braced against a nearby wall.

Worthless old man, he thought. If I were still with my gang, we'd put you out of your misery. Raj turned his back to the man and stepped forward in the long line when, out of nowhere, a familiar voice called his name. Raj looked back at the beggar, startled.

"Raj!" the voice repeated from beyond the blind man. Suddenly, a fellow employee grabbed his arm.

"Are you going to the movie, too?" Raj asked the young man.

"Not this one, Raj. I'm going to *The Cross and the Switchblade.*"

"The what?"

"It's a movie playing over at Mark Buntain's church on Royd Street."

"Who's Mark Buntain?"

"He's a preacher, probably the kindest person I've ever met. He feeds children and helps the sick. Would you like to go? I'll introduce you to him."

"No, I'm not interested in hearing about some god tonight. I want to see Clint Eastwood. He's my favorite actor."

"Yes, but you'll like this movie better," the friend insisted, "because it's about *you*—drugs, alcohol, and fights."

"I don't think so."

"C'mon, Raj."

Raj hesitated. "Well, if I can't see Clint Eastwood for some reason, I'll come over to the church."

Raj's Christian friend smiled. "I doubt that you're going to get tickets, because God wants you to see the other movie."

Ten minutes later, the shrinking line in front of Raj dispersed. The Eastwood attraction had sold out. Raj considered another movie, but he was ultimately drawn to the church by his friend's parting comment: "God wants you to see the other movie."

How Could It Be True?

In front of the church a tall Caucasian was trying to corral the crowd. Raj decided this must be the preacher his friend had spoken of, for a tide of teenagers swarmed around him as if he were a movie star. Parents leashed onto the hand of their young children. The mob spilled into the street.

"I'll never get tickets," Raj said softly. "There are too many people."

"It's free," said the young man standing next to him. "You don't need a ticket."

"In that case, if you want in, follow me," Raj blurted. He started to barge through the crowd, then reminded himself that this was a church. The doors opened and the crowd behind Raj conspired to push him inside anyway.

Raj didn't feel like he was in a church or a theater. Several kids behind him were spitting, the sound quality of the film was not as good as the cinema, and the screen was not as large. "At least it's free," he consoled himself.

As the movie progressed, Raj found himself liking the Nicky Cruz character who happened to be the leader of the gang. He admired his toughness, his boldness. But he was disappointed when the star converted to Christianity. Raj could think of more realistic endings, such as having David Wilkerson caught in the middle of another gang war.

"How could this have been a true story?" he questioned, descending the church steps.

Meeting an Old Friend

As Raj was getting ready to leave, he saw a former member of his gang sitting on a railing outside the church.

"What are you doing here?" Raj asked.

"I go here," the young man said.

"What?"

"Yes, this is my church."

"I never knew you attended church."

"I became a Christian a year ago. I met Mark Buntain, and he showed me the way to Jesus Christ."

Although amazed that his friend was now a churchgoer, Raj had no interest in hearing about his conversion or anymore about this white preacher. He quickly changed the subject.

"Where's Manaj keeping himself?" Raj asked.

The former gang member licked his upper lip and blinked twice. "Nobody knows, Raj."

Raj's face flushed. "What happened?"

"He was beaten up by some guys, then I think he landed in jail." The friend paused. "I only wish I had a chance to tell him about God."

"He has his own god," Raj reminded.

"I know, but I mean the true God."

"Who?" Raj teased. "The God mentioned in tonight's movie?"

"Yeah. He's real, Raj."

"He may be real, but He's not for me."

"How do you know? You don't know much about Him, do you?"

"Enough to know I don't need Him," Raj replied.

"Come with me to Sunday school and find out who God really is. Come and listen to Pastor Buntain speak. It will change your life."

"No, not Sunday. That's the day I'm going to go to the Eastwood movie."

"Just once. Come on," the young Christian urged.

He Died for You

Raj reluctantly agreed to visit Mark Buntain's church—primarily to silence his persistent companion. And, to his amazement, that Sunday he felt power he had never experienced. He even saw persons smiling, reaching over their seats to hug one another.

The white man who had wrestled with the mob at the movie was now bobbing and weaving behind the pulpit. Raj could not understand why this preacher moved his body so much and talked so fast. Still, it was as if this Canadian, Mark Buntain, had seen Raj's entire life. The stories he told, the scriptures he read—they all applied to Raj.

"If you want to be happy, stop fighting, stop using drugs and alcohol, and start following Jesus," Mark said. "He died on a cross for you. They nailed His hands to that cross. He allowed them to drive those nails through His palms to show you how much He loves you. In return, all He asks is that you serve Him. He loves you. We love you."

Raj's heart beat faster as he weighed the preacher's words. He could sense the white man's love. Then his mind flashed back to scenes in the Nicky Cruz movie. He could see himself as Nicky, the vicious street fighter with no conscience to curb his hatred.

But how can I be like Nicky . . . and be sure God exists? he wondered. I am an evil person. Raj shut his eyes tightly. "God, if You're real, take away my lust for alcohol, drugs, and cigarettes. I'm tired of hating, tired of fighting. How could You love me? I've never done anything for You. I've cursed You and hurt many people. I am nothing like this preacher. Why would You want me?"

Crying Out for Mercy

A week passed before Raj could bring himself to seek the white man's help. It was midday when Raj knocked on Mark Buntain's door, but there was no answer. In the chapel, Raj could hear a children's choir rehearsing. He sat in the rear and listened, hoping Mark would return soon. He gradually moved closer to the front and began humming along. The children and the director were singing and laughing at him simultaneously. Finally, the music teacher invited Raj to join them on the platform.

Standing on his tiptoes, a small boy dressed in a blue outfit whispered to Raj, "Hey, this choir is for kids."

"I know," Raj said, bending over, "but I *am* a kid."

A feisty smirk appeared on the boy's face. "Then what's this?" he asked, tugging vigorously on Raj's thick beard.

The assault on his beard, although it drew no blood, reminded Raj of his life with the gang. The fights, Manaj, the drugs—a flood of grisly memories swept through his mind. And yet, Raj the murderer, the drug addict, was now contentedly singing in God's house with grammar-school children. And for some unexplainable reason, Raj knew this was where he belonged.

After the choir dispersed, the chapel was unusually quiet. Mark still had not returned. Raj sat alone in the sanctuary and stared at the cross hung on the wall behind the pulpit. Then he studied his hands and imagined the pain Christ endured on the cross.

"God, can You forgive me?" he asked in a whisper. "Forgive me. Forgive me. Forgive me," he began to sob and speak louder. "Forgive me. Forgive me. Forgive me!" A teacher rushed into the sanctuary to see who was making the desperate pleas.

But Raj didn't care. He wouldn't have cared if his father, Manaj, and a thousand friends were in the sanctuary watching. He would have cried and pleaded for God's mercy anyway.

CHAPTER FOUR

Moti

A dusty Wurlitzer organ showered chords throughout the sanctuary as stained-glass windows sent rays of blues, greens, reds, and yellows over the congregation. The parishioners, meanwhile, sat reverently in the Gothic oak pews. Wooden beams stretched across the ceiling where hanging fans and lights were strategically placed. A large ceramic crucifix hung on the wall behind the platform, and statues of various saints lined the perimeter of the cathedral.

The congregation stood as the priest and his entourage began the processional. The priest wore a white satin cassock and a headdress that reached to the heavens. Gold lace trimmed his starched white gown. A brass headpiece on his staff reflected the golden rays of the sun.

Wearing a simple black robe, Moti carried a brass cross and walked several paces ahead of the priest. The ornament divided the boy's face into four sections as he approached the altar. Moti's mother cherished this portion of the liturgical service more than any other. How she relished every step her son took. Each mother wanted her son to be a cross bearer for the church.

"Moti was baptized as a baby and dedicated to God. Now he is serving God," she whispered to herself. "God will bless us because of our son."

After he performed his liturgical duties, Moti's mother would draw her slight, fourteen-year-old joy to her breast and kiss the top of his shiny black head. "You are such a fine boy!" she proclaimed.

Moti, however, found little satisfaction in his "holy" position. Being a cross bearer made his family proud—enough reason to continue for a few more years, he supposed. As far as Moti was concerned, the only advantage was his access to the communion wine. He and the altar boys comprised a small clan of saboteurs, frequently lifting a bottle or two for their own consumption.

Tempted with Power

One of the altar workers, Kalu, graduated from petty theft to witchcraft in the years that followed. He served communion in the church on Sunday and performed witchcraft throughout the week.

"Moti, do you want real power?" Kalu asked one day.

"I . . . I," the slender, thin-necked young man mumbled, not knowing how to respond.

"Let me teach you where to get power," Kalu interrupted.

Moti was reluctant. For years he had concealed his vices from his family. Witchcraft merely would make the charade more difficult.

"I can't," Moti resisted. "I am about to be married. My family is Christian. They wouldn't understand."

"They don't have to know, Moti. Let me show you how you can become wealthy with these powers," Kalu implored. "You can give your wife and children many new things. I need an assistant, someone to help me. Come with me at midnight. You'll see."

Moti finally conceded. When he was a young boy, Moti's mother had told him witch doctors were evil and powerless. Kalu, on the other hand, now claimed to possess the power to grant prosperity—or poverty. Moti was curious.

But his curiosity turned to regret when Kalu revealed their destination: the burning ghats where bodies were cremated. Even though Moti had passed by the place many times before, he had never gone inside. As he inhaled the putrid air, his stomach rebelled, spewing brown liquid on his tattered sandals.

"You'll grow used to it," Kalu beamed. The tall, dark Indian had larger lips than most natives and tightly coiled hair. "You'll be okay."

Moti dried his lips with one swipe of his forearm. "Why do we have to go inside?" he asked, feeling as if he might vomit again.

"That is where we must be to receive the power."

Moti's head ached. "I don't think I want anything to do with the ghats."

Kalu swung open the gate and motioned Moti to follow. "Come on!"

"I want to leave," Moti's voice broke.

"Just follow me," Kalu instructed. "Everything is all right."

"I am not all right," Moti explained in a whisper.

"We'll leave in one hour," Kalu promised.

Casting Curses

The witch doctor made his way through the courtyard, surrounded by towering trees and octopus vines that strangled the wire fence. The young men reached a corner of the yard where Kalu emptied his knapsack. He placed a necklace made of what looked like human fingers around his neck and slipped bracelets over his wrists. He stepped out of his pants and began prancing around the yard wearing only his cotton pullover shirt.

Moti trembled as he stared in disbelief. He thought about running for the gate, about fifty feet away, but his sandals were stapled to the earth.

A few minutes later, the witch doctor returned to his bundle. He removed two eggs with unusual markings and placed them on the ground. Again Kalu danced. After burying the eggs in the soil, Kalu rose and began flinging his arms in the air wildly, chanting unintelligibly.

Moments later, Moti brushed his hand through his hair, glad that the ritual was over. "What is it you have just done?" he gasped.

"I have just cursed Narwal," he smiled.

"Why did you do that?" Moti implored. "He's our friend!"

"Don't worry, it is nothing serious," Kalu assured. "He'll be ill for one day. Then tomorrow night we'll dig up the eggs bearing his name and he'll be well again."

Moti was not convinced. "Are you sure?"

"I've done this many times before. He'll be fine."

It Must Be Real

Moti had difficulty sleeping on his pallet that evening. He could feel every pebble. Each shrill howl of the wind sounded like the angel of death streaking past his ear. Tonight he had tasted the spirit world. It intrigued him. But tomorrow he would know if it was indeed real or just Kalu's imagination.

Narwal was not at the cathedral to fulfill his duties the following day. Where might he be? Moti asked himself. The skeptical young man hoped it was just a coincidence.

As if he knew what Moti was pondering, Kalu answered him. "He's sick, Moti."

"I'll find out for myself," he said sharply.

"Yes . . . do," Kalu said. "But be sure to meet me at midnight so we can make him well again."

Narwal, Moti discovered, was suffering from a fever. "It must be real. If Kalu can make him well by tomorrow, it is real," Moti concluded.

The moon resembled the half-shut eye of a god. Moti felt exhilarated by the mere sight of the ghat because of what it represented: power and authority. Now even the stench was bearable. The gate opened and the two spiritists entered their sanctuary. A naked Kalu danced and chanted before uncovering his treasure. He then continued to dance and chant.

"Come here," Kalu ordered.

Moti's feet moved cautiously.

"That's it. Closer! Now repeat after me."

Moti stood over the eggs as instructed and babbled confusing syllables. "What is it I said?" Moti asked.

"You said the spirits are your gods and asked that they give you power to heal your friend."

Moti felt betrayed. Kalu had misled him into saying something he feared would make the Christian God jealous of the other gods.

The following day Narwal returned to his duties at the church. Kalu proudly proclaimed his triumph as he and Moti polished the staffs and brass emblems with a white cream.

"Now do you believe?" the witch doctor asked.

"Yes, I believe, but I must see more." Moti's tone was firm.

"You will. You'll see things you've never seen before," he claimed confidently, prompting Moti's heart to accelerate.

"Kalu," Moti asked, "how is it you receive money from these powers?"

"I will show you tonight if you come to the ghat."

Moti nodded.

Intoxicated by Power

As Moti began his mile and a half journey to the ghat that night, he felt incredibly light—as if he was being carried by a winged creature.

As he darted down the street, he passed a shirtless baby girl crawling over her distressed mother lying on a doorstep. Moti was so obsessed with his adventure he paid little attention. He felt as though he was being ushered onto a throne, a place from which he could pronounce judgments of death or fortune. He wondered if what he was doing was contrary to the Christian way.

For a moment he felt guilty but decided, "I want power, not Christian ritual." With that, he jumped the fence surrounding the ghat.

Kalu already was inside. "Come, Moti, sit here," he instructed. Moti noticed a chilling, haunting quality in his friend's voice. "I will show you how to use these powers for wealth."

Moti stared at his young teacher.

"Tell me the name of someone with many rupees that you dislike," the witch doctor commanded.

Moti could think of no one.

"Very well, I will suggest someone," Kalu straightened. "The food merchant who owns the samosa* stand has money. Remember, as boys we often asked him for a few fritters? He just scolded us. Remember?"

"Yes," Moti closed his fist.

Kalu continued his demonstration. Moti watched intently as the witch doctor painted the man's name on the egg and began the ritual.

"Do you have any questions?"

"How long do these curses last?"

"Days, three months, six months, a year, or forever."

* *samosa:* a snack made of fried potatoes that are covered with flour.

"You mean this can cause people to die?" Moti swallowed.

"Yes," the man said without emotion. "If you enter the house of a dead man, however, you will lose all your power. Do not go into the home of a newborn baby or enter a cemetery, either."

"Why not?" Moti was puzzled.

"I will tell you another time. For now, just believe it because I say so."

"What about the vendor? How long is his curse?" Moti looked worried.

"Three months, but if he pays us, he will be unharmed."

A week later Kalu and Moti decided to visit the man's home.

Although the merchant's house was not extravagant, it was much finer than to what either of the young men were accustomed. Electricity illuminated every room, and for the first time in his life Moti saw a brass bed.

The vendor was asleep. His body was stiff, as if he had been removed from a casket. A ballooning stomach under the blanket was the only sign of life. The man's wife nudged his shoulder, and he immediately recoiled from his corpse-like position. He yawned and squirmed before noticing their unfamiliar faces.

"Who are you?" he murmured.

"We are witch doctors. We have placed a curse on you. If you do not give us three hundred rupees, you will die," Kalu said.

"Why have you done this?" he rasped angrily.

"We only do what the gods tell us. You have displeased the gods," Kalu explained.

Instantly, the man somersaulted from his bed. "Here, take this money and remove your curse," he begged, casting what appeared to be new bills into Moti's hand.

Moti returned home that evening with one hundred rupees. Never had he received so much money. "It was so easy," he mused. "I must learn more from Kalu." And that he did.

Terrified and Tormented

In the coming years, Moti continued to practice witchcraft. With his additional income, he no longer resorted to gargling the country's illegal, often polluted liquor. He could now afford the finest intoxicants in Calcutta. His wife, Ravina, and five children knew nothing of his cultic practices or of his allegiance to the powers of darkness. They were aware only of his devotion to alcohol.

Moti often drank alone at the ghat, oblivious to the stench and debris around him. The ghat was his domain. He felt comfortable there—until one night he thought his life was in danger.

Even in his drunkenness, Moti noticed that the fog seemed to rise from the red dirt inside the ghat courtyard. Moti's vision was blurred by the cloud layer as well as the whiskey that rushed through his veins. His chin was unshaven, his hair matted in swirls on his bobbing head. Suddenly, Moti thought he heard someone speak his name. His bottle crashed to the ground.

"Moti," a voice growled inside his mind.

He wanted to run, but the wire fence had become a cage, and the alcohol had rendered him helpless and confused.

"Moti," the voice snarled again.

Moti shook his head to stop the inner voices. "Who is it?" Moti trembled. There was no answer. "Kalu, is that you?"

"Moti," the voice resounded.

Moti's eyes blurred further. He wondered if he was just experiencing another drug-related hallucination. Regardless, it seemed real enough, for out of the smokey mist emerged a figure.

Moti stared at its scaly, swamp-green skin draped loosely over its bowed extremities. The nose on the monstrous face consisted of two holes that looked like they might snort flames at any moment. The creature's mouth and eye cavities were blood red, foaming with murky saliva. Splotches of hair like braided strings flared from its scalp.

"Moti," it laughed.

"Are you real? What do you want?"

"You," the demonic image spat. "Take your life, Moti. There is no more happiness here for you. Kill yourself."

The haunting voice continued lobbying for Moti's life. The witch doctor shuddered as the voice grew louder. He thought the entire planet was being juggled in the demon's palm and the ghat was about to collapse.

"Moti, Moti, Moti!" the voice taunted. The young man shrieked as he backed into the fence. Then, with one leap, he was in the street running, seeking asylum.

Although Moti never knew whether it was a hallucination or not, he didn't have the courage to return to the ghat for nearly a month.

An Answer to Prayer

Moti's wife, meanwhile, had begun attending the services at Mark Buntain's church. Ravina had received Jesus as her Savior, and she yearned for Moti to accompany her to the church that had given her new life. But her husband repeatedly broke his promises to visit, choosing to consume an "energizing" bottle of whiskey rather than to listen to a "powerless" priest.

"This Sunday, why don't you come with me to church, Moti?" she asked.

"A priest can tell me nothing I need to know," he resisted.

"Pastor Buntain is unlike most priests. God speaks through him. People are healed."

"I don't have time."

"Please, come this one time."

To put an end to her pleading, Moti said, "If I feel like it, I'll come." He returned to his bottle.

But when Sunday arrived, Moti was elsewhere. Tearfully, Ravina lumbered out the door alone. She considered it a privilege to walk to church down Park Street because it was so nicely paved. Most of her walking was done on uneven dirt roads. As she passed the graffiti-covered cement wall of a secondary school, her thoughts turned to her husband's drinking and his broken promise. Weighed down with discouragement, she stopped to rest against the wall.

"He's drunk more than he's sober," she grieved. "Oh God, please make him come with me to church someday. He needs You. Oh, how he needs Your help!"

Ravina could hear thunderous singing and clapping as she climbed the steps to the church. She was grateful to find a seat. Pastor Buntain, in his customary shirt and tie, was leading songs and worship with his hands raised. The radiant face of the preacher always mystified Ravina. Some Sundays she would find herself just admiring Mark

Buntain's mannerisms of worship while the congregation was praying.

She had just opened her eyes when a small man slipped into the pew and settled beside Ravina, resting arm to arm. She was mildly annoyed at the man's nudge—until she recognized the smell of his breath. Moti had just sat beside her! He had been drinking, but at that moment Ravina didn't care. She was just thankful to have him in God's house.

Ten minutes later Moti rose to leave. But, like a man on a treadmill, he could gain no ground. Ravina clutched the back of his shirt. The harder *he* pulled, the harder *she* pulled. For fear she would tear his clothing, Moti surrendered.

The Compelling Voice

Mark had preached for nearly an hour when he asked members of the congregation to lower their heads. The words from this preacher pierced Moti like darts, each sentence painfully slicing through the alcohol and lodging in the crevasses of his mind.

As Mark prayed, Moti wept like a child. A series of pictures began flashing through the man's mind, documenting the wicked life he had led. Suddenly, as if someone was speaking from inside him, he heard a loving, comforting voice, unlike the one he had heard in the ghat.

"Moti, I died for your sins. I rose again for you. I gave My blood and body for you. Won't you follow Me?"

Is this really Jesus? Moti wondered.

"Follow Me," the voice said. "Follow Me, follow Me, Moti."

Moti was terrified, yet filled with awe. "Yes, Jesus, I will follow You. Forgive me," he said, standing to his feet.

Mark and Ravina placed their hands on Moti's shoulder. "Jesus loves you," Mark smiled.

"Pastor, will you pray to God that I will not make Him angry?" Moti asked. "I am a bad person."

"Yes, I'll pray with you. God knows everything about you. He'll help you."

Moti felt as if Jesus Christ Himself had placed His hand on his shoulder. The power Moti sensed nearly buckled his knees; shivers streamed down his spine. Instantly, his body and mind felt purged of alcohol and all demonic temptations.

Ravina never again smelled alcohol on Moti's breath. Never again did he miss a church service in favor of an appointment with Satan or a bottle. But he did return to the ghat one evening.

A More Powerful God

"Kalu," Moti called crisply, as his friend began emptying his bag. "This is wrong."

"What'd you say?" Kalu frowned.

"This is a lie. This power is evil. This is Satan's place, his power."

Kalu studied Moti's face, bewildered by the sudden change. "Go away, Moti, before I curse you."

Moti did not budge. "Let me introduce you to a more powerful God."

Kalu ignored the offer. He began chanting his mantras as Moti tried to capture his attention.

"Kalu! Kalu!" he called. Eventually Moti turned, pledging to speak to Kalu another evening.

Moti returned to the ghat a few weeks later. Kalu was not there; another witch doctor was. An anklet of bells rang from his feet. Huge bones hung from his neck, and his hair was glazed with blood, milk, and water. Red spittle oozed from his mouth.

"The gods want you to give me five rupees," the man declared.

"You and your gods are liars," Moti rebuked. "Can't your god give you five rupees? Your gods want you to beg for money? What power is that?"

The witchdoctor's nose crumpled back as he snarled and grit his teeth. He began making rhythmic arm motions in Moti's direction.

"*Your* gods *take* blood. *My* God *gave* His pure blood. You need Jesus," Moti said boldly, unaffected by the witchdoctor's gyrations.

"The gods will destroy you and your family."

"Satan cannot harm me!"

Moti calmly watched the man rave and dance. Finally, the witch doctor, dripping with sweat, backed away.

"Please, sir, leave me," the writhing man began to beg. "Your God is more powerful than me. Leave me, please!"

As Moti walked away into the darkness of the unlit streets, he could almost hear the demonic spirits jeering from behind the fence. A few steps further, Moti, undaunted, looked up into the starless Calcutta skies as if talking into the face of God.

"Thank You for having mercy on me . . . for sending Mark Buntain . . . for revealing Yourself to me . . . for dying on the cross for me," Moti prayed.

His mind flashed back to his days as a teenage cross bearer and those dreaded processionals. How he had detested his black gown, the brass cross, and the liturgical services.

Now, for the first time, Moti understood the significance of the cross and how it was a symbol of God's power. Oh, how he wished he could do it all over again.

CHAPTER FIVE

Gopal

The people in the auditorium rose to their feet. Their tailored silk suits and designer dresses had padded their chairs for more than an hour while they had listened to the deities sing through a Hollywood-faced young man. Now it was their turn.

The ovation rumbled like a continuous explosion. Chandeliers in the concert hall vibrated; the ceiling and walls were unable to confine the noise. Children in the streets ran to the entrance, hoping to see what was sure to be a king or president. Flowers, currency, and pieces of jewelry smothered the stage as Calcutta's aristocrats continued their salute.

The young vocalist, smartly dressed in a European-cut black suit, bowed and smiled. The applause continued long after the curtain fell. Slipping through the slit in the curtain, the singer again acknowledged the ovation. "Gopal . . . Gopal. . . Gopal!" the crowd chanted.

Gopal's fame was mounting. He had the stunning good looks of Clark Gable and the mellow voice of Perry Como. Newspapers and radio stations predicted stardom for the local celebrity. One columnist wrote: "He has the voice no one can grow tired of."

Arrival in Calcutta

It had not been an easy journey to the crest of success for the young man. When Gopal was a baby, his father had died of an undetected disease. Gopal's uncles had swindled his mother, Sushi, of all her possessions and threatened to harm her and her baby if she refused to cooperate. Rather than confront her tormentors, she fled with little money and stowed away on a train to Calcutta. Gopal had just begun to walk and eat solid food when he and his mother embarked on their frightful pilgrimage.

The train had not traveled far when mother and child were discovered hiding behind a bin of grain.

"What have we here?" the stout railmaster asked sternly. The woman did not respond. "What are you doing here?" he yelled.

The woman gripped the baby tightly, hoping the man would show compassion for her and her child.

"Why are you here? Are you trying to escape payment?"

"I have no money," she said softly, casting her troubled eyes downward.

"Then you must leave the train," he said.

"But we cannot."

"You must!"

Sushi's eyes searched the man's haggard face, hoping he would not thrust them from the moving train.

The baby squawked, squirming in his mother's arms.

The man ceased his cross-examination as if he had just noticed the child. "You may ride to the next station, but from there you must find your own way."

Sushi thanked the railmaster by joining her palms together and hugging her chin to her sternum. The man never returned to carry out his threat. At each station more bodies piled onto the roof of the train. After a day's journey the locomotive arrived in Calcutta. The mother and son descended unnoticed.

Undernourished and Unemployed

Calcutta was like a foreign country to Sushi. She had never seen so many beggars in one place.

The rail station must be where they congregate, she thought. How dishonorable it is to beg when one can work.

Sushi suddenly realized that she and her baby had no place to go themselves. Sushi had no friends in Calcutta and no one to stay with until she found work. Her bag contained only a blanket and a few scraps of food. As the sun slowly descended, Sushi searched for a vacant patch of ground. Her son, strapped to her back, was bending her weary spine when she discovered a secluded spot between two stacks of bricks.

"This will be fine until tomorrow. Then I'll find us a home," she told her son. The young mother situated the baby's head under her bag and doubled the blanket on top of him. Her exposed arms were trembling as she nestled beside the warm bundle. She squirmed as two fist-sized rats brushed against her legs, the commotion setting off the baby's wailing vocal cords.

The following morning, Sushi labored from door to door asking for work. Gopal was taking a toll on her frail back. "No, no, no—we have no work," echoed in her ears between doors. Gopal cried for nourishment, but the scraps of food were gone. Even Sushi's breasts were barren.

The skies were growing dark at midday. Sushi knew she would have to abandon her brick fortress because it had no ceiling. The rains were titillating Sushi's skin when the smell of boiling rice steered her to a pile of boards and plastic. Its residents, three desperate children, rescued her from the elements and offered her food that Sushi figured had been stolen. Like cats they lapped goat milk and pawed kitchri* into their mouths. The hut was damp, unlit, and unventilated. But it was shelter, and Sushi was grateful for it.

Day after day, door after door, Sushi's plea for work was rejected. Nothing. Almost nothing.

"Yes," said the balding man who answered his door with enthusiasm in his voice.

"Hello, good sir. Do you have any work?"

The man scoped her from feet to forehead. "Please come in." Sushi's heart swelled. "What is your name?" he asked.

"Sushi," she said, admiring his wall hangings.

"Sushi," he repeated. "I like that name." His hand rubbed her bare arm. She looked at him peculiarly.

"What work do you have?" she asked politely.

"Much work, but I would like to get to know you first," he smiled. His hand slid down her arm again.

"What is the work?" she said, withdrawing from his touch.

"Like I said, there's much to do, but let's get to know one another first."

---

* *kitchri:* a soup-like dish made with rice and dahl—a small Indian bean.

She soon realized his intentions and skirted out the door, leaving the man casting insults at her back.

Sushi's tiny toes were blistered and her knees swollen from the many blocks she had traveled. Her braided pony tail had unraveled, and her hair lay in strings on her back. A patch of unoccupied cement was a welcomed sight for Sushi's tired legs.

From there, she watched a threesome take turns bathing under a hand-generated water pump. Another man squatted in a corner to relieve himself. The foul odor of open drains and smoldering ashes suddenly assaulted Sushi's nostrils. A shepherd was dashing from one side of his herd to the other, swatting sheep to keep them from straying.

"If only I could find work!" she thought. She now understood why there were so many beggars. Even skilled laborers had difficultly finding jobs for pay in this city.

Finding an Open Heart

The monsoon's thrashing eased one afternoon, leaving water to stagnate in the streets. Sushi pulled up her saree, waded through the slush, and knocked on a door.

The dingy yellow door cracked open. "May I help you?" a pale-skinned woman asked.

"Do you have work? My baby is hungry, and I am willing to work," Sushi pleaded.

"What can you do?"

Sushi sensed an understanding ear. "I can cook, mend, and wash. Please, ma'am, my baby is hungry."

The woman's smile widened. "Where is your baby?"

"He is staying with some children in a bustee."

"You do not have a home?"

"No, ma'am."

"How do you eat?"

"We eat with the children."

The woman's smile disappeared. "Bring your baby back with you. I will let you work for me."

"Bless you, ma'am." Sushi curtsied awkwardly.

The woman, Miss Rose, had come to Calcutta from Australia to work as a teacher. Her hair was rolled up in a ball, her skin smooth for a woman in her mid-fifties, and her eyes full of life.

While Sushi washed the evening dishes, Miss Rose read the Bible to Gopal and taught him songs. Sushi worked quietly, listening from the other room. As years passed, the full-cheeked boy grew and began to understand more of what his adopted grandmother was reading. He listened; he owed her that much. Miss Rose had given him and his mother adequate food and a mattress to share.

Discovering His Gift

When Gopal was eight, Miss Rose sent him to boarding school. There, in quest of pleasing Miss Rose and his mother, the boy excelled. Often he returned home with his report card raised high. Ceremoniously, Miss Rose rewarded Gopal's efforts with a kiss on the cheek and two biscuits.

During the school's morning chapel services, Father Smithson routinely led the boys in prayer and singing. Gopal's enthusiasm for music was noticeable. His voice rang out above the others, his facial expressions as happy as that of a birthday boy.

Other children mocked Gopal's singing, occasionally launching a paper missile at him during chapel. "Gopal's a girl," they snickered. "He sings like a girl."

Gopal tried to ignore them, but more and more students were making him the object of their taunting.

While his classmates played in the yard one afternoon, Gopal sat alone on a mound, tossing pebbles and humming songs Miss Rose had taught him.

"Why aren't you playing?" asked Father Smithson, approaching from behind.

"I want to be alone," Gopal said, trying to discreetly dry his tears.

"Why?"

"I don't know."

"Is it that you think you have no friends here?"

Gopal stared at a pebble in his palm. "I just want to be alone, that's all."

"I've heard you sing in chapel. You sing well." Gopal gave no response. The priest continued, "I have scheduled you to sing next week."

Gopal jolted to his feet. "By myself? In front of the other students?"

"Yes, next Tuesday."

"I've never sung by myself before," he said with obvious trepidation. "Besides, everyone will laugh at me."

"Don't worry about them; Father John will practice with you," the priest assured, patting the boy's shoulder. "And listen, Gopal. Just remember, we're your friends. We care what happens to you."

The boy's frown disappeared as the priest waddled to the aid of a scraped knee in the playground.

First Solo

The following Tuesday, minutes before chapel was to begin, Miss Rose appeared at the foot of Gopal's bunk bed. She clutched a shopping bag in her hand.

"Miss Rose!" he announced, dropping from the upper mattress with a thud.

"How's my boy?" she asked, her arms spread.

"Good," he said, his words muffled by her hug.

"Here are some new clothes for you. I wanted you to look your best today."

The lad tore open the package like a lion after raw meat.

Gopal's navy blue socks were stretched up to his knees, exactly matching the color of his shorts. His white, short-sleeved shirt was crisply pressed and his blue tie tied perfectly. As he marched to the front of the chapel with his back rigidly arced, Gopal thought the sides of his parched throat would stick together. He eyed the slender accompanist and swallowed hard.

Father Smithson smiled. Miss Rose winked and offered a quick prayer. In the back row Gopal's schoolmates were kicking one another—until he began to sing. Soon every ear was immersed in the music of this nine-year-old who had the voice of one twice his age.

Students and teachers clapped. Miss Rose nodded her approval above her busy hands. Since Gopal had never been the recipient of such applause, he felt uncomfortable with the ovation. The youngster stood frozen for a few moments before he was able to return to his seat.

Cultivating the Talent

Later in the day, Father Smithson intercepted the boy on his way to lunch. "Gopal, that was well done."

"Thank you, sir." Gopal tried to avoid a lengthy conversation by not breaking stride.

Father Smithson caught his arm and gently swung the boy around. "God has blessed you with much talent. What do you want to do with it?"

I'm only nine. What does he mean? Gopal thought. The silence was becoming awkward when the boy spoke up. "I'm not sure, Father. I like to sing, but I'm not sure I'm good enough."

"Of that, I am not sure either. One day would you like to find out?"

"What do you mean?"

"Would you like further training if it were possible?" Gopal was still confused. He didn't know how to answer. "Think about it, son," the priest added.

During the next several years Gopal faithfully performed for chapel services and special gatherings. And Father Smithson never forgot his proposition. He enrolled the student in a higher education program. There, the budding adult's skills progressed so well the priest made it possible for him to be near his mother and attend the Conservatory of Music in Calcutta.

While at the Conservatory, his reputation flourished. Gopal was besieged with requests from agents, radio and television managers, local officials, and restaurant owners. "You'll be rich very soon," his friends at the Conservatory predicted.

Dejected and Dissatisfied

To no one's surprise, the ovations became louder, the audiences larger, the financial rewards greater. Nevertheless, Gopal walked away from packed auditoriums dejected and dissatisfied. Fans crowded around him, but Gopal did not see them. His thoughts were clouded, injected with sheer depression.

"What's wrong?" a friend at the Conservatory asked, noticing a scowl on Gopal's face.

"I don't know exactly. Everything is going so well, but I'm not happy."

The friend chortled. "I'm the one who should be unhappy. I haven't had the breaks you've had. My music isn't earning money."

"It's not the money. I enjoy singing and writing songs. Getting paid for it makes it even better. But my music has to be for more."

"What more is there for a musician?"

"I don't know. Maybe this is just a phase. Maybe I'll get over it, but . . ."

"You will, my friend," he promised. "How about going for a drink?"

"No, I can't. I'm singing at a special church event tonight."

The friend laughed again. "A church! Why waste your time with a church meeting? They don't pay much."

Gopal flashed back to Miss Rose and the Bible stories she had taught him. He remembered the day she hugged him goodbye, just before she boarded the plane for Australia. The friend could see Gopal's thoughts were elsewhere. His eyes were glassy.

"Well, I hope it goes well tonight, Gopal," the friend said, excusing himself.

Gopal smiled halfheartedly with a slight nod of his chin before returning to his daydream.

A Unique Performance

Gopal had heard of Mark Buntain and his church, yet he knew little about either. The platform was a little higher than what he was accustomed to—more detached from the audience. That didn't matter. For those few minutes, the audience was his, regardless of the conditions. His music would melt them as it had so many times before.

Yet, Gopal still was astonished the white preacher would even invite him into his church. I'm not a devout Christian, he thought. Maybe this man thinks I am.

"Gopal, thank you for coming." Mark grabbed his hand as if they were old acquaintances. "Is that voice of yours ready to glorify God?"

Gopal avoided an answer. "Thank you for having me."

"Let's thank God. He's the One who brought you here tonight." Gopal peered away from the man's striking eyes.

Mark firmly placed his hand on Gopal's shoulder, then prayed, "God, use Gopal tonight to show Your people Your greatness. Bless every song, every word, every note, and may You alone be glorified."

Gopal closed his eyes. He could feel the blood rise to his face as the white man prayed. I'll be glad when I leave here, he thought.

Before Mark ended his prayer, an orchestra seemed to erupt from the auditorium. As Mark and Gopal advanced onto the platform, Gopal noticed a guitarist adjusting an amplifier and a drummer banging the cowhide covers that surrounded him. The pianist, his tie loosened and his hair feathered on the sides, was pounding the keyboard.

The songs were foreign to Gopal. He was embarrassed by his lack of participation in the service, but he clapped along anyway. Never had he seen so many enjoy music without having alcoholic beverages to loosen them up.

I wonder if all these people attend church here or if they have come especially to hear me? he thought.

Having shed his dark suit coat, Mark approached the pulpit.

"It's an honor to have Brother Gopal with us this evening. Many of you have heard him sing at other places and know the talent God has blessed him with." Made somewhat uncomfortable by the pastor's introduction, the young man stared at the top of his shoes. "Please welcome Gopal to our church," Mark said, his own hands clapping.

As Gopal played his harmonium and sang with his familiar vibrato, many in the congregation bowed their heads.

What have I done to offend them? he thought. They must sense I am not of their faith. His mind raced as the music flowed. I wish Miss Rose could be here. She would like to see me here.

As was his custom, Gopal held the fermata at the end of his final song for nearly a minute. Normally this left audiences in awe. Fans would rise to their feet in appreciation, but nearly everyone seated in the first few rows of the sanctuary had closed their eyes. A woman on the right was holding her red saree with one hand and lifting the other toward heaven. There was no applause. Just prayers. Somewhat bewildered by the response, the artist returned to his seat.

God's Songs Last

Following the service, Gopal found himself shaking hands and thanking appreciative listeners. Mark Buntain himself waited in line to visit the young man.

"Gopal, God wants to use you. I know you have a successful career going and you're on the verge of an even greater career, but God has a different plan for your life," Mark said. "A better plan."

The young man tensed, trying to think of something to say. "I'm still searching for the right situation."

"This is the right place. Will you come and teach here?"

Gopal would have laughed had he not seen the serious look in Mark's eyes. "I don't think that's possible. What about my career, my popular music? I can't walk away from that."

"God wants you here. Think about it. Then come and see me," Mark said, grabbing Gopal's right hand. "Gopal—God's songs last."

As Gopal's taxi exited the church gate that evening, radio speakers, seemingly planted closely to Gopal's ears, echoed the pastor's remark: "God's songs last, God's songs last, God's songs last." He heard those words time and again as the vehicle zigzagged through the city. Gopal flipped the wide lapels of his jacket up around his neck, trying to decipher what the preacher meant. He was in deep thought when the driver quoted the fare: "twenty rupees."

Four weeks passed. Attempts to write love songs ended in crumpled paper and sleepless nights. Again and again the wind whistled: "God's songs last, God's songs last." Gopal's lyrics were empty of meaning, the melodies repetitious. Leaning against the wall of his studio, he turned away from his instrument.

"I just want to sing my songs," he said, striking his fist against the door. "God's songs last," he heard in his mind again. "Is he saying that my songs don't last, that they're forgotten?" he said out loud. His brief tantrum subsided. "Maybe Pastor Buntain is right. I'm tired of just making people feel good for a few minutes. I want my music to stay with them. To last, to help people—like Miss Rose helped me."

Gopal found the preacher the next morning watching a woman stir vats of dahl,* a yellowish soup.

"Hello, Gopal! What a surprise!" he smiled, the steam from the pot fogging his glasses.

"Hello, Pastor."

"We're behind schedule. We must have this food ready for the children shortly."

---

* *dahl:* an Indian lentil bean soup.

Gopal was nervous, unsure where to start.

Mark spoke again. "What's on your mind, friend?"

The young man focused on his expensive leather shoes, then glanced at Mark's rubber soles. "What did you mean when you said 'God's songs last'?"

"What do you think I meant?"

"Well," Gopal breathed deeply, "I think you're saying that my songs don't really help people, that I'll never be happy until I do."

The cook, meanwhile, lifted her oar out of the pot, oblivious to the conversation surrounding her.

"I think you know what's right," Mark said softly, staring warmly into the young man's eyes. "And I have a position for you in our school when you're ready."

Wrestling with Temptation

Gopal's decision to work at Mark's school and give up his secular music bewildered his friends and professors at the Conservatory: "You're taking a big step back. Why give up all you have? What about your career? It's a mistake. Look at the money you're going to lose. Why can't you sing for the church and at your old places?" they urged.

Word of his new position swept through Calcutta. Some fans thought he had vanished, moved to London or New York. Requests for radio and television appearances dwindled, and soon Gopal was no longer recognized on the streets or mobbed by devotees. Instead, he spent his days teaching children in a secluded classroom. Whenever he heard a song he once sang or encountered a friend he studied with, Gopal wrestled with the temptation to return to the entertainment industry.

There, at least, many more people heard my music, he often thought. *These children are too young to appreciate my voice and my songs.*

A message arrived one day from a director of a Bengali film corporation, soliciting Gopal to sing the lead song for an upcoming movie. The young teacher rushed to Mark's office, hoping to receive the minister's blessing.

"Pastor Buntain, this message came for me today," Gopal said, handing it across the desk.

Mark examined the note with a blank face. "This is flattering. This man recognizes your talent."

"Yes, I guess so," Gopal said with a cautious grin.

"So does Satan, Gopal." The young man immediately slumped in his chair. "He wants you to sing your old music again. He knows it will pull you away from God, earn you lots of money, and make you famous. He also knows then you won't bless people or glorify God with your music.

Those children out there need you," Mark gestured. "Our church people need you."

The young teacher wrestled with himself for a few moments, calculating his rebuttal. "I know, Pastor, but can't I do both?"

"We both know it wouldn't work, don't we, Gopal?" Mark patiently awaited the singer's response.

The arms of Gopal's chair wrapped around him like the arms of God, refusing to let him make a mistake.

Gopal nodded his head. "Thank you, Pastor. Thank you for your time."

A few moments later, Gopal peered into an old trash bucket in the hallway and watched the last piece of the shredded message flutter to the bottom. That simple act of surrender finally fixed his commitment to Christ—one he would never regret.

CHAPTER SIX

Tara

Tara's soft down mattress was of the finest quality in India. Only the elite could afford such a prize for their children. Each of the three daughters had her own room decorated with the most elegant vases and sculptured furniture north of Coimbatore. Paintings on the walls would have made New York art galleries envious. The girls' clothes were made of silk, their jewelry made of precious metals—embellishments foreign to most children in India.

The coconut and prawn business had been lucrative for the Chacko family. Tara, at the age of eight, knew little about her family's fortune. She just knew there was nothing she could not have. Every weekend meant another bracelet, earring, or doll from her visiting grandparents.

Adorned with the jewels of royalty, Tara was the Chacko's three-and-a-half-foot princess. Servants were afraid to neglect even her most menial request. Her classmates, however, were jealous of her flaunted estate. Thus, they were not saddened by her sporadic attendance at school.

"God Is Going to Heal You"

Asthma often attacked Tara's lungs, making it difficult for her to breathe. Her condition baffled the finest specialists in the country. Treatments and experiments solved nothing. The family resolved Tara would never breathe normally.

A Christian neighbor, a double-chinned British woman, invited the young girl into her house one afternoon. She prayed for Tara. Nothing happened. The little girl continued to gasp for breath.

"Tara, I still believe God is going to heal you someday," the plump old woman said. The little girl beamed. She didn't tell her family about the prayer because they warned her not to speak to the woman. Tara's family was offended by the woman's religious propaganda and persistent proselytizing in the community.

Tara was nine when she heard loud voices and music booming from the woman's Victorian-style house. She crept closer to investigate. The neighbor was swaying back and forth with one hand raised—like we do in school, Tara thought. A light bulb directly above the woman shone like a spotlight. Her chin-neck wobbled like gelatin as she sang. A lean Indian man held a black book in his hand; another lady played an accordion.

"God, whoever You are, please take away my disease," Tara whispered. "If I get a chance to learn more about You, I will. But please help me."

Within several days the child forgot her conversation with the heavens. Months later, however, the family physician, after shifting the stethoscope across her rib cage, marveled at the improvement. Each checkup brought more encouraging news. By the time Tara was ten, the asthma attacks had ceased.

Shattered Dreams

The sun was in recess one July afternoon. God seemingly painted a gray ceiling over the earth. A cavalcade of automobiles stopped in front of Tara's two story villa. Relatives filed inside, their heads bowed, seemingly reading the grooves in the sidewalk. Women wiped their watering eyes. Tara's mother sat in front of an open window, the cool breeze drying her tear-streaked face. Men were drinking tea and talking business. The family had just returned from the grave of Tara's father, who had died of a sudden heart attack.

Tara studied her mother's frightened eyes. If only everyone would leave us alone, Tara thought. I can care for Mama. Their tears only make it worse. The young girl's secret wishes mounted when her uncle rose from his chair and strolled over.

"You must get married, Tara," he declared, pointing his curved finger.

"But her father wanted her to be a doctor," the child's square-faced mother intervened, deliberately brushing a strand of hair from her brow to avoid eye contact with her brother-in-law.

"That's impossible. She has two younger sisters, and Tara must be married first."

"She is only fifteen. Her father would never approve," her mother snapped.

"This is what is best for the family. Since my brother's death, the creditors have become nervous. This may place our business in jeopardy. She has no choice. After all, you were married when you were eleven. Your daughter will adjust as you have."

Tara waited for her mother to come to her defense, but no further arguments were offered. Tara's mother darted into her plush bedroom, her hand covering her eyes. Tara followed.

"What can I do, Mother?"

"I'm sorry. There is nothing. You must get married."

"I don't want to marry," Tara said, tumbling onto her mother's plump mattress.

"You must obey the family's wishes."

"But what about your wishes? You're my mother. I want to stay here with you."

"I wish that were possible. I'm afraid your uncles would not allow it. We have no choice."

Tara studied her mother's eyes a second time before deserting the house. Her feet stomped into the dirt, forging deep footprints. Galloping past the neighbor's house, Tara turned to see her uncle climbing into his foreign sports car. She wishfully slapped his face a hundred times.

Bridal Plans or Business Deal?

On a pleasant summer day Tara's uncle maneuvered his red sports car into the driveway. She recognized the three-piece, pinstriped suit. "Maybe he has changed his mind," she thought.

His lavender suit clashed with the red silk couch, his gold ring sparkling conspicuously, his cologne smelling like air freshener.

"I have come here to announce your engagement, Tara. I know you will be pleased. He's a twenty-two-year-old businessman from Calcutta. We have agreed upon a dowry,* and he'll be here next month to meet you."

"When will the ceremony take place?" Tara's mother inquired.

"Maybe in several months—if he wishes."

* *dowry:* the payment made to the groom by the bride's father.

Tara hoped the man would find her unattractive and unsuitable for marriage. But she knew there was little chance of that. Townspeople said she had the figure of a Paris model with the face of an Arabian princess. She had received her first proposal for marriage at twelve.

Her father vehemently vetoed any motion for marriage then because he was determined to have a doctor in the family. "Tara has more than beauty," he had said. "She has a gifted mind that must be developed."

When the young bachelor, Barhu, arrived, he kissed Tara's hand like a knight bowing before a queen. His mustache was trimmed neatly, leaving a thin gap between his upper lip and hairline. His suit inferred no sign of affluence, although it was clean and shapely. His ears were tucked under dark blades of hair, and a mole hung like a star at the end of his left eyebrow.

"It is a pleasure to meet you, Tara," he said, bowing his head slightly. Tara managed a smile, her lips securely closed. "Shall we go for a walk to get acquainted?" he asked.

Tara walked with her hands clasped together in front of her. Dust from the trail soiled her ankle socks and white shoes. She coughed a few times to hint her displeasure. Barhu launched into a boastful discourse on his career, allowing Tara to occasionally slip in two-word phrases when he paused for a breath. Mostly, she just nodded and smiled politely.

The family anxiously awaited the couple's return. From afar, Tara's uncles kept the couple under surveillance, hoping for a chuckle or smile, some suggestion that Barhu was satisfied.

"Tara is a fine woman," the visitor announced. "She does not talk much, but she is very beautiful. Let the wedding plans begin."

Tara's mother scurried down the steps to hug her daughter. The uncles grabbed for Barhu's hand. For them, arranging a marriage was no different than closing a business deal. Tara, however, detested their agreement. She had been sold like a slave girl to a man who wanted her as an employee and bed partner. Neither love nor her wishes were taken into consideration, and she despised her uncles for it.

Is This the Man I Married?

Not long after the wedding, Tara realized her husband was a different man than the one who had made such an impression on her family. The prince had become a dragon.

"Bring me some more wine!" he yelled. "Tara! Bring me some more." The girl trembled as his voice trumpeted. "Where are you, Tara? More wine!"

His friends held their glasses up as Tara set another bottle on the table and quickly retreated. Cigarette smoke cast a haze over the room, making the picture of Jesus on the far wall indistinguishable.

"Damn it, girl," he bellowed, pounding an empty bottle on the table, "we need more wine."

Tara approached apprehensively. "We have no more wine."

Barhu shoved her from his path. "I will find it," he slurred, scattering empty bottles onto the tiled floor.

Tara curled up on her bed, praying to "Most Precious Mary."

A flame smoldered inside her as she visualized the faces of her uncles and husband. "They have done this to me. I was once wealthy and respected. Now I am nothing more than a slave."

New Freedom in Christ

One afternoon a British woman invited Tara to go with her to church. Desiring not to disappoint or insult the woman, Tara agreed to attend one Sunday.

The choir sang for twenty minutes. For Tara, the music was refreshing, a far cry from the liturgical hymns of her church and the blaring noise of the Rolling Stones heard in the streets. Tara clapped and smiled as the congregation sang. A hearty man in a shirt drenched with sweat bounced from side to side on the platform. He would have appeared deranged had others not been rejoicing in a similar manner.

"That is Pastor Buntain," the English woman commented, pointing to the pulpit.

"He enjoys singing," Tara tittered.

"Yes," the woman joined in.

"Does he sing well?"

"Probably long ago. His voice is not as strong as it once was. Sometimes he preaches five times on Sunday." Tara shook her head in disbelief. "He is a good man. He helps many people."

Something about this white man kept Tara's eyes glued to the pulpit. He wasn't like her uncles and husband. His words were kind and gentle. She saw sweat saturate his shirt and soak through his tie. He applied his handkerchief to his face every few minutes, unable to halt the splash of perspiration.

His words spoke of a Jesus she had never known—a personal Jesus who wanted to care for her, not condemn her. "I cannot worship this Jesus. My family would never accept me," she said, trying to contain herself. "They know only their way."

"Come and kneel at this altar," Pastor Buntain compelled. "Jesus is waiting for you to make a decision. Do you want to know the Lord I am speaking of?''

One would have thought Tara was carrying a football the way she bolted through the crowd to the altar.

"Father," she looked up at Mark. "Forgive me for I have sinned."

"There's no need to tell that to me, dear. Tell Jesus. He's listening," Mark smiled.

Moments later, Mark was leading the petite woman in a prayer. Her British friend knelt beside her, one arm draped over Tara's back. The woman wept as she heard her Indian friend ask: "Jesus, will You come into my heart?"

Answered Prayer

For more than a year after her salvation experience, Tara's religious statues remained in an uncovered box under her bed. During that time she never missed a church service. Then, one Sunday evening, as javelins of electricity hurled across the sky, Pastor Buntain noticed that her usual seat at the end of the fourth pew was vacant. He and others wondered about her absence when someone passed a note to the pulpit. It read: "Tara called, baby has fever, please pray."

As her baby's temperature rose, Tara's faith diminished. Have I angered God by removing the statues? she asked herself. Maybe I should put them back. The young woman grabbed for the musty box under her bed when suddenly her eyes were drawn to a Bible on the chair. The woman seized the Bible and placed it next to the baby's head.

"God, help my baby," she prayed. "Please take away this fever. Make my baby well."

By morning the baby's temperature was normal. Tara slid the box of images further under the bed, knowing her personal God had answered her prayers.

Tragedy Strikes

Tara enjoyed long, eventful days with her four children, making up games and teaching them Bible stories. One day their playtime was interrupted when a neighbor boy barged into the house.

"Come quick! Shammi has been hit by a car!"

Tara dropped the plate in her hand. "Where is he?" she asked frantically as horrible images of her son rushed through her head.

"At the old people's place. I'll show you." Tara trailed the boy to a private nursing home. A grizzled man squatted on his heels next to the wooden table on which Shammi lie. A woman wearing a turquoise smock stood at the boy's feet, her hands mysteriously at her side.

"Are you a doctor?" Tara asked.

"No," the woman said softy. "I am a nurse."

"Where is the doctor?"

"There is not one here." The woman held her head down.

"We must get a doctor," Tara cried. She moved to grab Shammi's arm.

The nurse blocked Tara's hand. "It is too late. Your son is no more."

Tara's legs crumpled beneath her at the shocking news. She awoke moments later with the nurse overshadowing her.

Tears began bleeding from Tara's heart.

The nurse said, "I'm sorry, ma'am. He was able to talk. They did not think he was seriously hurt. That's why they brought him here instead of taking him to the hospital."

"Do you know what happened?" Tara asked, unconcerned with brushing the tears from her face.

"He was struck by a car and was brought here by some friends. That's all I know."

Tara staggered to her feet, bellowing. "No! No! Shammi, you *can't* die!" She screamed and cried uncontrollably.

The nurse squeezed the woman's arm, trying to calm her. The residents already were rustling in their beds. "I'm sorry," the nurse whispered. "Would you like someone to walk you home?"

Slumping in agony, Tara wailed, "He can't die!"

An old man with a puckered forehead crept out of the room, unable to cope with the noise. Another attendant and a doctor who had been summoned appeared in the doorway.

Tara's face was drawn, her pupils hidden by the gushing tears.

"Please sit," the doctor said as the nurse gently pulled her arm down.

"Shammi! Shammi!" Tara mourned.

The nurses and attendants were relieved to watch a syringe filled with medication temporarily relieve the grieving mother.

Sympathetic words could not ease the months of suffering. Tara's thoughts were a cesspool of nightmares: Shammi leaving the front door, his body under the car, his bleeding head.

Barhu added to her depression, blaming his wife for the "murder" of their son. "Why did you allow him to go? It's your fault," he reminded her at the dinner table, snatching food from the children's plates between stinging words.

Tara did not retaliate. She merely prayed silently that he would not beat her tonight as he frequently had in recent weeks. His vicious slaps often bruised and disfigured her face. Suicide had become more attractive, sleeping without fear more difficult.

Domestic Violence Erupts

Then one day it happened. In a fit of rage Barhu's hand lifted as the obscenities tumbled from his mouth. Tara braced herself. Like a club, his palm creased her nose. Blood canaled down the brim of her upper lip into her mouth, and a seething Barhu crashed out the door. Tara lifted herself from the brown rug and telephoned Pastor Buntain.

"Pastor," she sobbed.

"Yes, Tara. Are you all right?" he asked, turning on the nightstand lamp.

"He hurt me again, Pastor."

"Are you all right?"

"Yes, Pastor. But I'm afraid he's coming back."

"Lock your door. I'll be right there."

The minister rolled back the covers. Huldah rubbed her eyes.

"What is it, Mark?"

"Barhu and Tara again."

"Get someone to go with you."

"I'll be okay," he yawned, pulling his pants over his pajamas, the tail of his shirt hanging out.

Thirty minutes later, Mark found Tara shivering, her eyes swollen from tears. The children were huddled together in the bedroom. Mark gathered the whimpering youngsters under his arms. "Everything is okay now," he reassured them. His comforting words were ridiculed by the sound of two fists rapidly assaulting the door.

"Open the door or I'll kill you!" Barhu yelled.

Mark sent the children into a secluded room and confronted a seething Barhu. The minister took a step backwards. Tara gasped.

"Why are you here?" Barhu challenged.

"To protect your wife and children," Mark answered.

"Get out of my house!"

"Barhu, *you* will leave or I'll get the police."

"This is *my* house, and you're not welcomed here."

"Get going, or the police will be here in a few minutes," the preacher warned.

A drunken Barhu thought for a moment. "I'll be back. Be careful, preacher." Barhu pedaled backwards.

A few nights later, neighbors beckoned Mark to Tara's aid once again. Mark pounded loudly on the door to override the deafening bedlam inside.

Barhu came to the door with his fists raised, threatening to kill whomever it was. "Why have you come again?" he sneered.

"God has brought me here to keep you away."

"This is my house, get away from here."

Mark whisked past Barhu inside. Tara's shoulders were against the wall. "Tara, are you and the children all right?"

"They're fine," Barhu snarled.

"Listen, Barhu, you get out and stay out, or I'll kill you myself," Mark growled.

Barhu's mouth unsealed. He glanced at Tara, then lunged past Mark as if to attack someone in the street. Mark scurried to lock the swinging door behind the fleeing attacker. Tara's bleached face found sanctuary in Mark's arms.

"Everything is fine. You're okay," Mark said, hoping his words were prophetic.

Barhu was not heard from for several months.

God's Sign of Protection

Tara pushed open the door and waved the children inside one afternoon. Her youngest daughter remained outdoors to swipe at a green lizard in front of the house. The girl was peering into a hole in the ground when Tara yelped and screamed, "God! What has happened?"

In their absence Barhu ransacked the house and stole the family's valuables.

Mark entered the room an hour later to find the children rummaging through broken glass, cracked furniture, and torn upholstery.

"Pastor," Tara asked, "why would God allow Barhu to do this?"

Mark searched his heart for answers. "I don't know why, but I know God has heard your cry and He will deliver you. He is with you. He loves you and your children."

"I know He does, Pastor. I'm just afraid for our lives. Will Barhu be back?" she stammered.

"I don't know that either," he said, wishing he could say 'no.' "But I'm confident that God will protect you."

"Look, Mama!" a child squealed excitedly. Tara and Mark wheeled around. The girl's tiny fingers were clutching a glass-framed picture of Jesus. "*This* didn't get broken."

Tara took the picture from her daughter's hands and studied it. Then she let loose with a wide, peaceful grin as she remembered God's promise: "I will never leave you nor forsake you" (Hebrews 13:5). For now, that was all Tara needed to know.

CHAPTER SEVEN

Chandra

Hari swerved from one edge of the sidewalk to the other, desperately trying to hold onto the sixteen ounces of pleasure in his hand. The wide stripes in the thighs of his trousers were soiled, the pants too large for his shrinking frame. A strand of rope kept them secured under his tattered T-shirt, his ragged sandals tied to his feet by strings.

Hari stuck his tongue in the bottle, then threw it down savagely. Shards scattered in every direction as Hari struggled through the crowd. The baby strapped to his back was too young to realize the apparent danger. Hari's feet were sliding under him as if on ice skates, his arms flailing to keep him upright.

Suddenly the haggard, middle-aged man crashed into a stack of crates. Struggling to his feet, Hari was oblivious to the purple lump forming on the baby's forehead. Like a caravan camel seeking water in the Sahara, the tandem wandered down the street in search of their home.

Hari began knocking on doors, hoping to find a familiar face. Reena, Hari's wife, met him at the entrance of their cubbyhole as if he were a disobedient teenager.

"Where have you been? Why did it take you so long? Where's our water? You mean you've been gone all day, and you didn't bring us water? Where are the buckets?"

Hari rolled his drooping eyes. He looked as though he were ready to sprawl onto the shredded floor mat.

"Answer me. Have you been drinking again?" she asked, moving closer to smell his breath.

Reena could see her words were not penetrating his consciousness. She guided her husband to his resting place, only to see two blue tickets protruding from his pocket. She lifted them to her eyes.

"The horses! Drinking and gambling. Why do you do this to us?" Reena was tempted to claw the face of her now-still husband.

The woman, gray beyond her years, left to aid Chandra, the youngest of eight children.

"What happened to you?" she asked, knowing the baby couldn't answer. "Did he do this to you?"

The mark directly above the bridge of Chandra's nose resembled a tilak, an oval shaped decal worn on the forehead by Indian women. Reena touched the bruise and glared at her snoring husband, resolving that never again would she leave her son in his care.

A few years later Reena would no longer have to worry about Hari's treatment of her baby. Hari awoke one evening sweating and vomiting. The oil lamps were lit, shedding a yellow tint onto Hari's already yellow eyes. He pointed to a bottle in his coat pocket. One of the children reached for it before Reena intervened.

"No!" she exclaimed, grabbing the bottle in mid-flight. "You're going to the hospital. No more. You've had enough liquor already."

At the time, however, she didn't realize the seriousness of his condition. Just hours later Hari's lifeless body was deposited on a coroner's table, surrounded by a dozen cadavers in the room. It strangely resembled a slaughterhouse.

"He died of alcohol intoxication," the coroner said to his aide, scribbling the findings on a clipboard. "I think he's the nineteenth this month."

A Defiant Delinquent

Thereafter, Reena's sister helped support the family, sending Chandra away to a boarding school. There, Reena's "jewel" became anything but precious. The Brothers running the school would have needed a fortress with a stockade to keep the boy confined. Enticed by theaters and bars, the ten-year-old carefully scaled the six-foot wire mesh fence. Then, during the early morning hours, he would sneak back into his room, usually undetected.

Only when Chandra began bragging about his exploits did the Brothers inspect his bunk more frequently. Each infraction translated into days of punishment—kneeling down in the corner of the dining hall while the other children played. Fearlessly, the stringy-haired boy showered the tile floor and corner walls with spit. Chandra chuckled at the mess he created, but his superiors paid no attention to his sinister laugh.

White scribbles and diagrams covered the blackboard, leaving the chalk tray full of white dust. Students' pencils moved rapidly across desk tops as the schoolmaster suddenly rose to his feet.

"Chandra, please stand."

"Why?" the boy retorted.

"Stand, now!"

Chandra climbed from his chair, brushing the hair off his ears.

"What are you are doing?"

"Nothing."

"Your eyes have been on the tests around you more than on your own. What explanation do you have?"

"I was just trying to see how many they were missing," he said with a familiar grin.

"If you were a good student, I might believe you. But your marks would rival a goat's." The Brother's chin stiffened. "Tear up your test."

"I haven't done anything. If you want it torn up, you do it."

The schoolmaster strolled to Chandra's desk with deliberate steps. "I said, tear it up."

"No," the boy snapped. The other children were wide-eyed.

"If you don't tear up that test, you're expelled."

Chandra couldn't back down in front of his peers. "I won't," he defied harshly.

"Listen," the master hissed, nudging the boy back into his chair, "you don't talk to me like that. As for this test and your education here, you better do a lot of praying."

Returning to Calcutta

The next morning Chandra lugged his bag onto a blue and white bus, destined for his home in Calcutta.

"You have disgraced this family," his oldest brother charged, backhanding Chandra's cheek. Chandra glared at him. "Why come back here—to disgrace us some more?" the brother yelled. "You were given a chance to make something of yourself. And you let us down."

Chandra peeked at his frightened mother. She braced herself for the escalating conflict and covered her face with her hands. "I didn't belong there. I want to live here," he shouted back.

"Yeah, well we don't want you," his brother retaliated. "You're just like your father."

Chandra again cast his eyes on his mother. She seemed to know what was about to happen. Her eyes begged him to stay, but it was too late for words. Chandra was gone.

The boy stayed awake all night. He had heard stories of what gangs and drunks had done to other kids on the streets.

He soon learned that by supplying cigarettes and drugs to a colony of addicts, he could safely sleep with them on roofs and park benches. But it wasn't long before Chandra was not only supplying; he was using. At the age of twelve, he was consuming more snake poison, pills, cigarettes, and ganja than he was food.

Turning to Crime

During the next seven years, Chandra's body demanded more and more drugs. Potions, powders, and pills left the young man's cheeks looking old, deflated, his eerie laugh frozen into a sneer.

Lurking in a cavernous alley late one evening, the young man tried to restrain his coughing and sneezing. Any noise could alert his victim. His eyes, as cold as glass, spied around the corner from inside his personal hell-hole. Chandra had resorted to using the knife wedged between his pants and belly-button to subsidize his habit.

"Give me your wallet and jewelry, mister, or you're not going to live," he whispered a few inches from a terrified ear, the knife held near the man's shaking neck.

The man's tailored suit was fraying against the cement wall. "Okay, let me go, and I'll give you everything," the man promised.

"This knife is sharp. I'll slice your throat. So hurry up, give it to me."

With his loot in hand, Chandra rushed to one of his dealers. Frantically, he counted out ten rupees and tossed the smack into his mouth. Chandra was nearly unconscious by the time he tripped his way into the gloomy basement of an abandoned building. Roaches scattered as he hunkered against a wall shared by three drug addicts.

A Convicted Criminal

Less than twenty-four hours after fleeing in a stolen motor scooter, the young man found himself in prison rooming with the depraved of Calcutta—about one hundred winos, murderers, rapists, and addicts. He was locked in a cell isolated from what mattered most: drugs and alcohol. Chandra hopped from one prisoner to the other hoping to deal himself a fix. He would even have bartered his clothes, but the cell was devoid of his chemical salvation.

Two days passed. Chandra wrapped his arms around his shaking frame, trying to control his spastic muscles. A black man with hairy ears and decaying teeth laughed at the young cell mate cradled beneath him. "I hope you die, boy. I could use a new pair of shoes."

The judge, garbed in his black gown, motioned for the policeman to begin letting the prisoners out of the "chicken coop" that afternoon.

"Chandra Rai!" the judge announced.

Chandra walked slowly to the base of the walnut-stained podium, his eyes too blurred to look into the judge's face.

"You have been charged with the theft of a motor scooter. Our investigation has found enough evidence to find you guilty. I sentence you to five months in jail. Do you have anything to say?"

The young man's eyes tried to focus on the ground, his head swiveling limply. "No," he grunted.

The judge banged the gavel and read another name. Chandra was barely coherent as the policeman strong-armed him back into the cage.

The spray of a cold shower that evening was as shocking as a dip in an Arctic lake. Chandra finally came to his senses. He could feel his skin tingle and his eyes awakening, just in time to catch a fellow prisoner stealing his pants. Chandra thrust his fist into the man's stomach and snapped the culprit's head back with a knee to the nose. The man's skull bounced against the cement wall, blotching it red. Three guards hurdled the comatose man and tackled a rampaging Chandra, his fists waving wildly in the air. In the end he found himself alone in a small, dark, square room.

A Second Chance

Flies were attacking Mark Buntain's oiled hair as he made his way into the prison facility. A stocky guard greeted the white preacher with the respect of a government official, ushering him into the presence of the local chief of police.

"Hello, sir," the chief said.

"Good morning, sir, how are you?" Mark replied.

"I am fine. How may I help you?"

Mark took a piece of paper from his shirt pocket and read the name: "I am here to see Chandra Rai."

The chief ran his fingers down the sheets on his desk. "Yes, here he is. Father, he is in confinement for fighting. Do you want a guard in the cell with you?"

"I should be okay. No thank you."

"Very well, take him to Corridor F, room number eleven," he ordered.

Mark followed a young prison guard through an iron gate. The footsteps of the two men ricocheted off the tight, windowless walls. Inmates hobbled to the small eye slits in their lead doors, hoping to hear the dangling keys of a guard coming to release them.

A spider web veiled Mark's face as he entered the dimly-lighted tunnel. The squeaking chatter of rodents and insects echoed in the hallway as if being broadcast through a loudspeaker.

"Rai!" the guard shouted through the slit. "Stand back! You have a visitor."

Mark knew he might be entering a cage with a Bengal tiger, yet he calmly said, "Hello, son, my name is Pastor Mark Buntain. I am a minister, a pastor."

The unshaven young man shielded his eyes from the light. "Why are you here?"

"A relative of yours asked me to come."

"My family doesn't even know I exist. They threw me out long ago."

"I know nothing about that. I just want to be your friend and to help you."

"Then get me out of here," Chandra raised his voice.

"That's what I want to do, but on one condition."

"What's that?" Chandra sneered.

Mark hesitated, noticing the young man's feet were bare. "You'll have to come to our church and join our youth program. It's a drug rehabilitation program. There you'll get clean clothes, a bed, and food. But I have to have your word that you'll stick with it."

Chandra slumped against the damp wall. "Okay. If you get me out, I'll come. I'll do anything to get out of here."

A large hand reached toward the boy to seal the agreement. Chandra wiped his crusted hand against his chest and gripped a white man's hand for the first time.

Broken Promises

Six weeks into his drug rehabilitation program, Chandra and a friend sneaked onto the church grounds after midnight. They broke through a glass door into Huldah Buntain's office. While Chandra watched and listened at the door, the other boy pried open the cupboard and cracked the safe. A few days later Chandra was arrested and sentenced to six months in prison for the incident.

"Chandra," Mark called through the cell bars, why did you do it? We had an agreement."

"Yeah, well that was your agreement, not mine."

"Our church youth program was better than this, wasn't it?"

Chandra shrugged his shoulders.

"When you're released, come and see me," Mark said. "Maybe we can find you a job and a place to stay."

Chandra turned his head away. "Maybe."

"Dear God," Mark prayed through the bars, "be with Chandra. Protect him. Let him know how much You love him and how much we love him."

While Mark was petitioning heaven in the inmate's behalf, the young man yawned, sighed, and coughed disrespectfully. It was his way of telling the preacher he wasn't interested.

Hopelessness and Despair

Rations of bread and water had been sufficient to sustain Chandra in prison. But when he returned to the streets, the addict was obliged to fend for himself. He was losing weight and growing weaker. His ribs poked through his skin; needle marks trailed up and down his arms. He was also suffering from diarrhea and a mild case of hepatitis. Living from injection to injection was becoming more futile for the twenty-two-year-old. Suicide made more sense than living, he thought.

One afternoon he closed his eyes and darted across a busy causeway, hoping that an on-rushing vehicle would help him escape his "life" sentence. Honking horns and bumpers seemed to pass right through him without harming his one-hundred-thirty-pound frame. Drivers yelled and swore at the crazed pedestrian. Three Japanese businessmen stared in disbelief. A rickshaw puller stopped his carriage and scratched his head.

The moon had begun its descent when Chandra wandered into the basement of an abandoned building. He stumbled over a body. It didn't move. Chandra looked down at the skeleton, reasoning that he, too, would overdose.

Ten capsules, a quart of liquor, and fifteen tokes of opium quickly took their toll. Fellow junkies laughed as Chandra fell prostrate on the floor. "Hey, Chandra," they nudged him, "what you on? Give us some." They laughed again.

Flirting With Death

Several hours passed and Chandra was nothing more than a mannequin. His friends could not wake him as the wind sneezed through a gutted window. Chandra's feet were dragging, his chin resting against his chest, as the two addicts put his scrawny, needle-freckled arms around their shoulders.

"I think he's overdosed," one said.

"What should we do?"

"Let's just leave him at his mother's doorstep. I don't want him dying here."

Chandra's mother was frantic. Her screams woke the entire neighborhood. Her boy was still breathing, but she had never seen him looking so ghostly. Feeling helpless and terrified, Reena examined her son's comatose body.

Hours passed without a twitch or mumbled phrase from her Chandra.

Three days later, Reena rose with the sun only to find her sons's body shaking as if he were having an epileptic seizure. Reena strapped him to the cot with her arms.

"Help!" she screamed. "Help!"

As if waking from the dead, Chandra opened his eyes.

"Chandra, you're alive!" Reena breathed deeply. "You're awake. We were afraid we would lose you." The boy continued to shake. "Can you hear me, Chandra?"

"Yes . . . s. . . . s," he stammered, clutching his mother's shoulder. He hadn't been held in someone's arms in twelve years. He could see the pain and joy in his mother's face. He knew she cared about him. And he wanted to be there with her.

"Thank you," Chandra said, closing his eyes again to bask in his mother's warmth.

Conversion of a Cynic

A girl Chandra had met at Mark's church convinced him to attend a summer youth camp north of Calcutta. Chandra was incapable of declining her mosaic, brown eyes and velvety lips even if it meant having to confront Pastor Buntain again.

While the young people gathered in a circle to sing and read the Bible, Chandra sat undetected on a distant rock and smoked a cigarette.

"Where were you?" the girl asked as he returned.

"I just went for a walk."

"Aren't you enjoying yourself?"

"I'm just not used to sitting and listening that much." To himself, Chandra was counting the hours until he could return to the city and a bottle of snake poison.

The service that night started like all the others with choruses and testimonies about God. "I wish they'd quit talking about God all the time," he said to himself. "I thought they came up here to have fun."

Teenagers encompassed him. They were crying and speaking to the sky like some of his Hindu and Muslim friends. "Everyone here is just getting emotional." He shook his head critically, realizing he was the only person with his eyes open. Many had fallen to their knees just to pray for Chandra and worship God.

Suddenly, an inner voice began to speak to the young man.

"Chandra, I am your Savior. Why don't you give your life to Me?"

Chandra thought it was his imagination. Was he getting emotional like everyone else?

"Come to Me, Chandra; I've been waiting for you all these years." The young man turned as if to leave, to escape the compelling voice.

Once again the voice reverberated. "I've been waiting for you. There's no need to run from Me any longer."

Chandra debated whether to run through the mass of kneeling teenagers between him and the door. The inner plea continued. Finally, Chandra could take no more.

"Jesus," Chandra cried, startling his girlfriend. "Make me clean. I need You to help me."

Chandra lowered his head, knowing something miraculous was about to happen. And it did. Intantly, his dependency on drugs and his desire for wicked pleasures left him. Chandra raised his head and opened his eyes to the smiling and tearing faces of a large group of young people surrounding him. The meeting quickly evolved into what resembled a high school pep rally. His new found Christian friends clapped and roared their approval and congratulated him with embraces.

Mark walked toward Chandra with slow, deliberate steps. After momentarily staring into the young man's tearful eyes, he threw his arms around Chandra and wept with him.

"You have made God and the rest of us so happy, Chandra," Mark said. "This is the beginning of a new life for you."

Chandra tried to thank Mark for his help but he was so emotionally broken that he could not speak. His arms could only squeeze affectionately the man who had escorted him to the foot of the cross.

A Transformed Life

Chandra was back in the streets a few months later, but instead of a knife, pills, or even a bottle, he carried a New Testament. Two friends listened in disbelief as their "fellow junkie" told how he had been instantly delivered from drugs and alcohol. They felt the fabric of his new shirt and inspected his styled hair.

"You want a few tokes?" his friend asked.

"No, it's not for me anymore."

"Can't you smell it? Doesn't it smell good?" he said, blowing smoke in Chandra's face.

"I'm not interested. I've got Jesus."

"What does Jesus have to say about ganja?" the boy teased.

"I don't know exactly, but . . ."

"Then, here, have a few. Remember how good it is?"

Chandra studied the brown wrapper, remembering its warmth and aroma. "No, I promised I wouldn't."

The junkie celebrated with a few more puffs. "C'mon, no one will know."

Chandra gnashed his teeth, fighting the temptation that sought to recapture his soul. "No, I can't. I'm a Christian now. I don't need drugs anymore, and neither do you. Jesus loves you. He wants to live inside you. All you have to do is receive Him."

"Your god lives inside you?" the addict laughed.

"He does. He helped me give up ganja, alcohol, and everything else. He can do the same for you if you ask Him."

The flabbergasted friend licked the rim of his bottle. "Why would I want to give this up? I don't want it to go away," the man slurred.

Chandra pulled the New Testament from his back pocket and handed it to the man. "When you're sober," Chandra said, "read this. I'll be back tomorrow."

Chandra was out of sight when the two addicts began wrestling for control of the valuable black book. Within minutes their dispute was settled, each agreeing that the book would earn enough on the black market to fill each of their needles with drugs to soothe their inner pains.

Chandra, meanwhile, walked the streets feeling better than he ever had, anxious to tell the people of Calcutta of the inner peace that can only be found by knowing Jesus Christ.

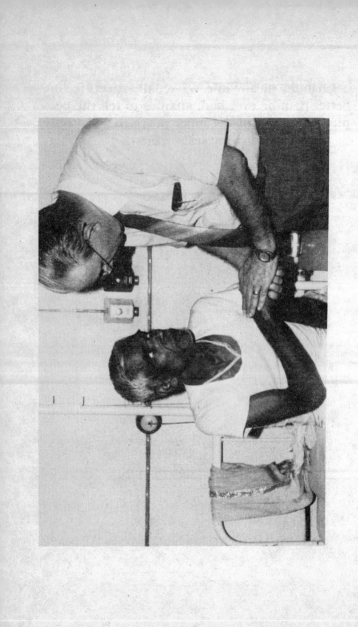

CHAPTER EIGHT

Krishna

As a little boy, Krishna had enjoyed "couching" up beside his mother. His small body fit perfectly between her knees and breasts. Her soft thighs and warm arms were comforting and made him feel safe. When she went to the market, Krishna swung from her limbs, occasionally grabbing an exposed vegetable or brass vase from the counter.

The taller Krishna grew, the more he idolized his mother. She was a goddess reincarnated, he thought. Her flowing black hair and pearl smooth skin complemented her enchanting smile. Those were Krishna's memories—pictures padlocked in his mind.

It was inconceivable that the coffin ten feet in front of him contained the remains of his beloved mother.

Earlier in the day the rangy, dimple-chinned boy had slipped into his slacks, the ones his mother had made by hand. Each hair was in place. Even his ears were clean. If she can see me from heaven,

I want to look my best, he said to himself as he straigtened his clothes and took a deep breath.

The coffin was nothing more than six pieces of pressboard nailed together. But Krishna paid little attention to the box. His sunken eyes were focused on the visage extending above its edges. He could see her rounded nose and red-gray lips.

"Move ahead, son," his father nudged.

"No," Krishna refused, pulling away. "I don't want to."

"Son, you must pay your last respects to your mother."

"This is not my mother. She is alive."

The line halted; the crowd could hear commotion in the front of the church.

"Yes, son, but you must not be disrespectful to her," his father said with a firm tone. "Just tell her how much you love her."

Krishna closed his eyes, trying to turn off the spigot of tears. His thick hair and narrow shoulders were drawn upwards as he made his way to the "death box." Each step was faster than the last. He bent over his mother's body, wishing he could revive her, praying the tuberculosis could disappear.

"Mommy, I love you. I miss you. You don't have to worry. Everyone here will be fine. I miss you." His father then guided the youth to a seat in the front row. Krishna buried his head in his father's chest only to catch a tear that had fallen from the man's starched left cheek.

"I miss her, too, son," his father, Lalsingh Mondol, replied, squeezing harder.

Krishna's two little sisters and younger brother began to cry as friends and relatives lamented over the coffin. Krishna placed himself between the girls and embraced their shoulders.

"Go ahead and cry. It's all right," he said to his sisters, peeking up at his father's tear-stained face.

As the funeral proceeded, Krishna's thoughts drifted, distancing him from the garlands of flowers, the eulogies, and music. He vaguely heard the soloist sing "How Great Thou Art," his mother's favorite hymn. In the pew behind him his aunt was nearly hysterical. Nevertheless, Krishna's daydreams became more vivid, more real. He could feel his mother hugging him before he left for school. Her voice was so clear in his mind. "Be good today, and learn more about Jesus," she would say.

He remembered hearing her pray at night when his father was working as a waiter in a nightclub.

"God," she had said, kneeling in a dark corner, "help my husband to know You like I do. Please help him to stop smoking and drinking so much." Every time she rose from her prayer stool, her face was like that of the angels Krishna had heard about in school.

He could still picture the night his father told Pastor Buntain he wanted to become a Christian. Krishna had never seen his mother so happy. She laughed and cried as she emptied her husband's bottles of alcohol onto the dirt road in front of their house. From that day on his father was a different man.

He remembered when the assistant pastor came to their home to drive his mother to the hospital. She was lapsing in and out of consciousness, her eyes opening and closing. His father laid her on the back seat and sped off, leaving Krishna standing in the street to watch the taillights fade into the Calcutta smog. He sat on the curb and wondered if he would ever see her again.

Two days later, Mr. Mondol had circled his children around him. "I have something to tell you," he had said, fighting the tears. "Your mother has gone . . ." He had trouble saying the last phrase. "Gone . . . to be with the Lord." Krishna could no longer control the tears damming up behind his lids. He hadn't had a chance to tell her good-bye, to tell her how much he loved her.

Questioning God

That thought hurled the teenager back to reality—to the funeral—to the front row seat of this horror movie. He could feel his back teeth grinding, his muscles tightening. Why would You take my mother from me, God? he cried silently.

Just then Pastor Buntain stepped forward, alongside the coffin. He cleared his throat.

"Funerals are joyous and sad occasions. We are sorrowful because we've lost a dear woman we all loved. On the other hand, it is a joyous time for Meeta because she is with our Lord. This woman exemplified love and diligence like few I have known.

"Some of you here today do not know the source of her love and strength. It was our God in heaven. Many of you here need to have a personal experience just like Meeta had. I encourage you to speak to me after the ceremony if you do not know our Lord Jesus Christ. Nothing would make Meeta more happy," Mark smiled, "than to know you gave your heart to Jesus today.

"Now let me turn my attention to the family," he said, peering at the weeping husband and four children. "God has placed a tremendous task on your shoulders, Mr. Mondol, and you, Krishna. These children will need a lot of love and care. On behalf of the church I pledge to you our help and support. We love you. You are part of this bigger family," he added, spreading out his arms.

Those words arrested Krishna's anger. But he still had many questions.

"Sir," he said to the assistant pastor driving them home after the funeral, "Why does God kill people?"

The young Indian minister thought for a moment, wishing he could turn around and speak to the boy face to face. "God doesn't kill His children. He doesn't *cause* them to die. He *allows* them to die."

"Why?" Krishna asked.

The minister thought again. "The Bible says, 'Everyone is appointed once to die.' As to why some people die now and some later, I don't know. That's in God's hands."

"Well, why do we have to die at all?"

Lalsingh interrupted. "We'll talk about this another time, son."

"It's okay," the preacher in his mid-twenties said. "If we don't die, we'll never be able to go to heaven."

"But my mother said that someday Jesus was coming back to take us to be with Him. So that means we can go to heaven without dying."

"That's the rapture, but many will die before that."

"Why? Why can't God take all families to heaven together?"

The minister's vehicle pulled up to the house. "We can finish our conversation on Sunday, all right?" he suggested.

But Krishna was not satisfied. "Can't we talk now?" he asked before his father scooted him out the door.

Adjusting to Loss

For the first time, Krishna viewed the family's two-room shelter as a jail cell. No light bulbs. No windows. Everything reminded Krishna of his mother: the old chairs his father had taken from the nightclub, the hole-infested couch, the blanket she had cuddled under at night waiting for her husband, the large metal pot she had used everyday, even the candle she had preserved from her wedding.

Lalsingh grabbed the pot and began boiling water. The children took off their Sunday clothes. Lalsingh suddenly realized he had inherited the family's cooking and washing duties.

Eventually, Krishna was drafted and trained to do the household chores. Lalsingh often returned home from work at midnight after a sixteen hour shift. The teenager would have his father's food waiting and his clothes laundered and folded for the next day.

"Thank you, Krishna," his father sighed, crouching to eat off the small crate-table one evening. "Are the children asleep?"

Krishna nodded.

"I have something to tell you." Lalsingh's lips quivered. "I received word today that your grandmother passed away."

Krishna felt as though the flesh was melting off his face. His nose dove into his sweaty palms. He didn't want to wake the children, but he was incapable of restraining his emotional eruption.

"Why is God doing this to us? We have done nothing to Him!" Krishna exclaimed.

"Son, this is not God's doing."

The children stirred and then wandered in minutes apart. "Grandma has gone to be with Mommy," Lalsingh told them. They, too, began to cry. The five of them huddled around the table, sniffling and weeping.

Sacrificial Giving

The sun had been down for three hours when Lalsingh arrived home the following evening. Krishna was mending his sister's dress when his father coughed his way through the door.

"How was work?" Krishna asked.

"Good . . . This is for you," his father said, handing Krishna a package.

Krishna approached the box cautiously. "What is it?"

"Open it."

By the look in Krishna's eyes one would have thought he had won the lottery. He admired the treasures in the box, then proudly lifted them high. "Keds!" he announced.

"It took me six months, but I finally earned enough extra money to buy them. They are strong shoes. They will last long."

"Thank you," Krishna grinned.

"Try them on. Do you like the color?" His father looked on with pride.

"Yes, they're perfect. Thank you, Father."

Before Lalsingh gave his life to Christ, he had merely been the man married to Krishna's mother. Nothing more. Krishna felt he was undeserving of being called "Father," and for years he had found it difficult to forgive Lalsingh for the sorrow he had caused his mother. "He's not good to her. I wish he didn't live here," Krishna often said to himself before his father's conversion.

For years Krishna had wondered if Lalsingh really cared for his mother. But now all his doubts had vanished. Krishna was certain she had been Lalsingh's only lover. After Meeta's death, Lalsingh had cried into his floor mat every night for weeks.

The teenager stared at his new shoes until he knew every thread. In the gloom of his mourning, the tennis shoes brought him pleasure. He wore them only on special occasions, knowing that when the rubber was erased he would not have another pair to replace them.

The Keds were no longer wearable by the time Krishna was seventeen. The heels and toes of each sole were riddled with holes. Besides, the boy's feet had outgrown the sneakers over the past three years. Many dreams had been collected in those shoes. Thus, like a prized mantlepiece, the boy kept them in a box under his three shirts and two pairs of pants.

More Bad News

Krishna was admiring his worn "old friends" one afternoon when a knock on the door startled him.

"Krishna!" a voice called.

Krishna cracked open the door. "Hello, Pastor and Mrs. Buntain."

"May we come in?" he asked.

The boy was embarrassed to let the Buntains step into their tiny home, even though they had been there many times before. "Yes," he said.

"Are your brother and sisters here?"

"Yes," Krishna responded, barking them into the front room. They stacked themselves in front of the Caucasian couple as if posing for a family portrait.

Mark himself had asked God why so much tragedy had beset such precious children. Their white teeth shined like pure milk.

"Listen to me carefully." Mark took the younger boy's hand. "Your father is sick, and he is in our hospital."

"What's wrong?" Krishna blurted.

Mark wished he could ignore the question. He despised his answer. "They've diagnosed cancer, but we're going to do everything we can to make him well."

Krishna knew cancer's death curse, but surely his father would survive. God wouldn't allow another death to attack their family, he convinced himself.

"Can we see him?" asked the girl hugging Huldah's side.

"Yes, yes . . . you'll see him soon," Huldah said, brushing the girl's hair from her eyes. "Krishna, we would like to put your brother in our boys' home until your father gets well." She sensed Krishna's trepidation. "Just until your father is well," she stressed, patting his arm. "We'll take good care of him and make sure you and your sisters are well cared for here."

"All right," he agreed. "I guess I must quit my classes and care for my sisters."

Mark said, "No, we'll send someone to help you. You just continue your studies."

A faint smile appeared on the boy's relieved face.

But Huldah was back at Krishna's door a week later. "Your brother is crying for you, Krishna. He really misses you. I have talked to your uncle. He'll take your sisters if you'll come and stay with your brother at the boys' home."

"Why can't he come back here?" the weary-eyed teenager asked.

"You have more than your hands full. Come now, all of you, get ready. Your brother needs you," Huldah ordered, carrying a loose pile of clothes to her car.

Lalsingh's Last Request

Despite its modern facilities, Krishna viewed the hospital as a cemetery. He likened the beds in his father's room to coffins. "I would rather die at home than be locked up with dying patients," he concluded. "Father doesn't belong here. He's not going to die."

When Krishna placed his hand on the bed rail, he found his father gazing through a window at the moonlight, absorbing the speckled sky.

"How are you feeling?"

"Fine," the man answered with a painted smile. "How are my children?"

"Good. Are you hurting?"

"No, I'm fine." The boy could see, however, that each breath was a painful task for his father.

"Krish . . . na," Lalsingh gasped in broken syllables. "Sit here . . . If I die, trust God . . . but go to the Buntains. They'll guide you. They've promised me they'll care for you. They'll love you as if you were their own son."

"I know, but Father," Krishna began to complain.

"Listen," he sighed. "Do as I say. Make us proud of you. We'll see you again someday."

"You can't die. God can heal you if He wishes. God won't let you die."

"I don't understand why I have this illness, son . . . but God does. Never question God. He loves us. God and the Buntains will have to care for you now. Remember, I love you, and we'll be together again someday."

The following day, Krishna learned his father had died just before daybreak.

Becoming a Big Brother

Krishna returned to class at the boys' home the following week. He spent his evenings on his bed dissecting the ceiling with his eyes. Every giggle in his room clanged like cymbals in his mind.

"How can they laugh? My life is so bad . . . and they laugh. Don't they care?" he asked himself, forgetting how young the orphans were.

"Hey, 'Krish,' " an impish boy called, peeking over the mattress as he stood on the lower bunk. "Do you want to play ball with us?"

"No, not today." The teenager turned away.

"Why not? We want you to."

"Well, I don't want to."

"We want you to. So come on," the little boy persisted.

"I'm . . ." Krishna was about to get angry when the kid's innocent face shot a cupid-like spear. "I'm not . . ."

"Come on, Krish," the puppy-eyed boy begged from under threadlike bangs.

Krishna ruffled the boy's hair and followed him out into the cement yard.

"What's your name?" Krishna asked.

"I know yours," he giggled. "Krish."

"No, it's Krishna. What's yours?"

"Sanjay," the boy said, grabbing the older boy's hand. "Will you be my brother?"

Krishna picked him up. The boy wrapped his legs around his new pal's back. "I already have a brother, but I wouldn't mind having another one. If you'll be my brother, I'll be yours." The boy began to celebrate and tell everyone in the play yard that "Krish" was his new brother.

In the months that followed, Krishna taught Sanjay to tie his shoes, make his own bed, and wash himself behind the ears. Krishna even broke up a fight or two involving his "little brother." Thus, it was a sad, disheartening day when Krishna was asked to accompany his companion to the airport for a flight to New York to join his adopting American family.

"Sanjay, I will miss you, but I will see you again."

"Krish, can't you come with me?"

"That's not possible."

"When will I see you again?"

"Someday," Krishna said, remembering so vividly his father's parting words.

"I know," Sanjay persisted, "but when?"

"I'm not sure, but I promise we'll be together again."

"Can it be next week?"

"I don't think so. You're going far away."

The boy squirmed in his car seat. "Is it as far away as heaven?"

"Not that far, but one day we'll be in heaven together," Krishna explained.

"When?"

"I don't know, but someday."

"I have something for you, Krish." The little boy removed a foggy snapshot of himself from his back pocket. "Do you like it?"

Krishna studied it from the passenger's seat. "Thanks, Sanjay . . . Remember, I love you."

"I love you, too," he giggled.

As the boy's plane lifted from the tarmac, Krishna stared at the out-of-focus photograph and daydreamed. He dreamed of heaven and being reunited with his loved ones. He dreamed of looking into the face of God and apologizing for blaming Him for taking his parents. He dreamed of pleading for God's forgiveness.

God looked down from His throne and said it was as good as done.

CHAPTER NINE

Munshi

It had been a strenuous day for Mark. He had spoken in three villages and prayed for cripples and babies whose stomachs were swollen with worms. The ride over bumpy dirt roads had jogged the vertebrae in his back, leaving him stiff and sore. Huldah was half asleep when he collapsed onto the mattress, still wearing his socks and white short sleeved shirt. A gentle rub of his arm signaled she was pleased he was home.

Huldah had an eventful day as well, arbitrating between two combative teenage employees and trying to locate enough funds to pay for next week's feeding program. Fortunately, the familiar noise of traffic from the street below wasn't enough to wake the Buntains from their sleep.

Always on Call

Suddenly, they both sprang from their pillows. The loud pounding sounded like someone was taking an axe to the front door of their flat.

"Who could that be?" Huldah asked. "It's after midnight."

"I don't know," Mark said, throwing on his robe. Mark recognized the man's face through the peep hole. "What's wrong?"

"It's Sunil. He's drinking again. You must come."

"Okay." Mark waved the old man away.

"Who was it?" Huldah asked.

Mark crawled back into bed. "It's our weekly visit about Sunil. He's drunk again. The same old thing. I think I'll just let them handle this one without me. Sunil doesn't want to change. And until he does, it's not doing either of us any good to babysit him."

Huldah rolled over on her side. "I think you're right. Good night."

Mark grabbed his robe twenty minutes later. This time Sunil's wife was at the door. "Please, Pastor, Sunil needs you."

Mark could hear the clouds colliding as he scurried down the stairs. A wicked storm was smothering the city. Drains were flooded. Fierce winds blew the rain at a forty-five degree angle. Autos stalled in the rising water.

Two policemen were staking out the building when Mark, wearing his cleric, arrived at Sunil's address. Horrifying screams echoed from an upstairs room. Mark's head was like a water-logged bird's nest as he started up the decrepit stairway attached to the side of the building.

"You can't go up there, Father," the officer ordered.

"I have to." The screaming intensified. Mark saw two feet sticking out from under the third floor railing. "Someone might be hurt. Let me go."

The policeman moved aside as Mark sprinted up the stairway as spryly as a twenty-year-old. Lying on the landing was a man, his bare feet hanging over the edge. Mark's fingers searched the man's neck for a pulse. The man was dead. Sunil and his wife were screeching and squealing inside the apartment.

"Shut up!" Mark demanded. "I'm here to help you."

The screaming persisted. "Shut up, I said!"

The woman seated on the couch gagged her mouth with her sleeve. Sunil was too drunk to understand Mark's instructions.

"Sunil, shut up!" Mark repeated. Mark's fist started from his side and whipped across the man's chest. Sunil fell onto the couch beside his wife. The police on the street looked at one another, then looked up the stairs.

"Are you all right?" one officer yelled.

"Yes, but this man is dead," Mark declared from the railing. "They said he was drunk and fell down the stairs."

Mark and a neighbor wrapped the body in a blanket and followed the ambulance to the hospital to explain the accident.

Mark crawled back into bed at four o'clock in the morning.

"What happened?" Huldah awakened.

"It's a long story . . . a sad case. I'll tell you tomorrow," he yawned.

"Do you have to go in early?" she asked.

"I have a breakfast meeting with a businessman that I can't miss."

"Who is it?"

"His name is Munshi. He's an executive for a large company."

"Can't you postpone it? You need your sleep."

"No, it's too important. I have a feeling God's going to do something special for this young man."

A Rebellious Youth

Munshi, the youngest of six siblings, had been reared in a religious family. His father was paid well for managing tea gardens, so Munshi never went without when he was a youngster. When his mother died shortly after his birth, Munshi's brothers and sisters became his unofficial guardians. By the time Munshi was five, his family was teaching him the ceremonial rituals, incense-burning, and the names and legends of their gods.

"Be good, study, work hard, and don't fight. Then you will make the gods happy," they preached.

Throughout boarding school and college, he never questioned the family's religion. But when he moved to Delhi to accept a position as a store clerk, Munshi began to change. There were no relatives to dictate his beliefs or criticize his behavior.

"Munshi, why are you sitting around? I told you to stock that shelf," squawked the store owner, gesturing his displeasure.

"I will. Just let me finish my cigarette." The twenty-two-year-old blew smoke in his chubby employer's face.

"*Now*, Munshi! Do it *now*," the owner swore. "I can't even talk to you anymore you smoke so much."

"Leave me alone. You're lucky I'm even wasting my time here. I could be making twice as much somewhere else."

The store owner retreated. He knew the boy was right.

Scorning Christianity

Munshi's skin was fairer than most natives, but his high cheekbones, deep eyes, and slender nose were unmistakably Indian. He knew his youthful profile and strong physique could attract any girl he wanted. He spent his lunches leaning against a street pole, eyeing Delhi's finest women.

Dusk frequently marked the beginning of an evening in a smoky bar. Rock music blasted as thinly-clad waitresses with pierced noses filled Munshi's glass every fifteen minutes. He wouldn't stop ordering until his slurring speech was unintelligible. Then, arm in arm, he and his buddies would dance their way home.

Munshi spent other evenings playing poker in his apartment. The players were immune to the nauseating smell of empty beer bottles and stuffed ashtrays. Their skin and clothes reeked as the dealer called for another game. "Who's in?" he asked, his sleeves rolled up over his elbows.

Five chips collided in the middle of the table. Munshi opened another bottle.

"I met a Christian on the corner who invited me to church today," one of the players said. "I told him he'd have to pay me ten rupees. And do you know what he did? He reached into his pocket and handed me five. He said I'd get the rest if I . . ." the young man looked down at his watch, "met him an hour and a half ago." The table broke into laughter. Munshi convulsed as he leaned back in his chair.

"Why do they bother?" Munshi said, taking another large swallow.

The friend was still cackling. "Because they want to give us money," he said, lifting a handful of chips.

Munshi said, "Seriously, they're trying to convert us. We don't infringe on their freedom of choice. Why should they belittle us?"

"They're just fools," another said. "It's better to ignore them."

"You're right," said the dealer. "Let's get on with the game."

Climbing the Corporate Ladder

After landing a corporate position with a company in Bombay, Munshi said farewell to his friends in Delhi. It wasn't long, however, before the playboy found new companions who shared his zeal for women, liquor, and gambling. His parties became more frequent, more bizarre. Senior executives worried that their prized junior executive was moving too quickly after hours.

"Munshi," the department head warned, "I'm worried about you."

"Why?"

"It has to do with the circles under your eyes and some rumors I've been hearing."

"What rumors?" Munshi perked up.

"Parties that last all night, drinking beer until morning."

"Ram, I'm only twenty-eight. I'm fine. Don't worry about me."

"Munshi, we just want you to slow down a little. You're not going to do the company much good, or yourself for that matter, by swimming in your liquor."

Munshi nodded his head with a boyish grin. "All right. I hear what you're saying, Ram."

That evening, guests congregated in his high-rise apartment. Munshi welcomed his visitors with a filled glass in each hand. "Enjoy yourselves," he said, glazed eyes simpering. When the party subsided, the handsome, young executive was slumped over his couch, dribbling into a cushion like a slobbering infant.

A year later, Munshi accepted an executive post with a company in Calcutta. His plush office on the twelfth floor symbolized his importance and success to his family and friends. The solid oak furniture, shag carpet, and penthouse view were more than the young man had ever imagined. The little boy who had once knelt before the family images and played in the tea gardens was now an influential businessman, rubbing shoulders with India's "jet set."

With his new wardrobe and sculptured hair, Munshi could easily have worked as a high fashion model. But he enjoyed the taxi rides through the cluttered streets, the one-hundred-rupee-a-plate dinners, and the high pressured board meetings. There wasn't a speck of gray in his hair, but his fellow executives listened intently to his shrewd proposals. He was gaining recognition and prestige among India's financial wizards.

As word of his company coups spread, Munshi's social activities became less important. Maybe it was maturity, new-found priorities, or possibly Calcutta itself. Either way, parties and bars appeared less attractive to the bachelor.

When he stood before a mirror, it was becoming more difficult for him to look himself in the face. The deceit and political schemes he employed had transformed his gentleman's face into that of a bloodthirsty warlord. He ate at the finest restaurants, and his apartment rivaled a Manhattan suite. Nevertheless, Munshi could only see the restless beast he had become, out to devour fame and fortune. And he hated himself for it.

Drawn by Curiosity

One morning on his way to work, he yelled to his driver, "Stop!"

The cab driver turned and squinted at his fare.

"What does that say?" Munshi pointed to a poster on a concrete wall. "Can you read it?"

The driver shook his head.

Munshi threw a ten rupee note into the front seat and hopped out into the sidewalk traffic. To his dismay, the sign said exactly what he thought he had read: "Peace through Christ . . . Come, discover what this means at 6 p.m. tonight, 18 Royd Street."

Munshi was curious. Later that evening, he followed the wooden planks over the muddied terrain to a large tent. The wind detoured raindrops from their course. The tarpaulin served as a large umbrella over the expectant crowd. Munshi stepped just under the canopy.

"Please sit down," an usher proposed.

"No thank you, sir, I'll stand."

"Please sit, be comfortable."

Munshi obliged. Soaring cars and sweeping winds made it difficult to hear the large Caucasian behind the microphone. The usher recognized Munshi's dilemma and invited him to attend the Sunday services.

Purposely, for weeks, the young executive filled his Sundays with other activities. But finally he could no longer ignore his inner cravings. The congregation was singing "Jesus breaks every fetter" as he approached the church. Dressed in a tweed suit, Munshi surveyed the audience.

They're singing something they believe, so sincerely, so loudly, he thought. But what does "fetter" mean to them? His thoughts were interrupted by the large white man's thunderous voice.

"God is good," the man rumbled. "We're so blessed to have each visitor here. I'll look forward to greeting you after this morning's message."

Munshi pondered Mark Buntain's sermon, especially his remark that each man must receive salvation from Jesus Christ. "I don't understand; somehow I must visit with this man," he decided. The young man made his way to Mark's side after the benediction.

Munshi asked, "Hello, sir. Would it be possible to meet you one morning? I do not believe as you, but I have many questions about your God."

"What's your name?" Mark asked.

"Munshi Biswas. I'm an executive for a large company here in Calcutta."

"It's an honor to meet you, Munshi. Can you come to my office sometime this week?"

"Certainly. When is a good time?"

Mark removed his calendar from his pocket. "How about six-thirty Tuesday morning?"

"Yes, yes, that will be fine. Thank you." Munshi smiled.

A Sincere Seeker

Mark's tie was cocked and his belt fastened on the wrong notch as he labored down the stairs Tuesday morning. The eventful evening with Sunil and the dead man had left Mark exhausted. Munshi was waiting as Mark brushed the sleep from his eyes. The two sat down in front of their sweetened tea, uncertain who should initiate the conversation.

"It was wonderful having you with us Sunday," Mark said.

"Thank you."

"What exactly did you have questions about?"

Munshi set his teacup down without a sip. "Sunday you said we must have Jesus in our lives, that only He can save us. What do you mean by the word 'save?' "

"Munshi, have you ever done something you knew was wrong?"

"Sure."

"Did you feel bad inside?"

"Probably. Sometimes."

"In some cases that is God telling us we have sinned. Instead of sentencing us to hell—an awful place—for those bad things we do, God sent His Son, Jesus Christ, to die and serve as a sacrifice for all the sins you and I commit. And as a result, everyone who is saved will live with God forever in heaven."

Munshi hung on every word. His teacup remained untouched.

"But in order to receive God's gift of salvation from the penalty of our sins, we must do three things: first, we must tell Him we love Him; ask forgiveness for our sins; and then serve Him."

"How do you serve Him?" Munshi asked.

Mark could see the young man's opposition to God wilting. After each scripture Mark read from his flimsy leather Bible, another question rippled from Munshi's lips. Two cups of tea later, Mark was still answering the businessman's queries.

"But how can I be sure I am a Christian?

Mark glanced at his watch. "It's almost nine. I've got to teach a class. I'll tell you what, Munshi, why don't you go home and read Psalm 103? I'll drop by your home later in the week, and we'll discuss your question further. Do you have a Bible?"

"No, I don't, but I will buy one."

"Here, take this one for now," Mark offered.

Munshi reluctantly grasped the minister's Bible. By even touching the book, he knew his life would never be the same.

As his cab dodged a line of neatly-dressed school children, Munshi's fingers rapidly flipped to the prescribed passage.

> Bless the Lord, O my soul; and all that is within me, bless His holy name! Bless the Lord, O my soul, and forget not all His benefits: who forgives all your iniquities, who heals all your diseases, who redeems your life from destruction, who crowns you with lovingkindness and tender mercies, who satisfies your

mouth with good things, so that your youth is renewed like the eagle's. . . .

The Lord is merciful and gracious, slow to anger, and abounding in mercy. He will not always strive with us, nor will He keep His anger forever. He has not dealt with us according to our sins, nor punished us according to our iniquities. For as the heavens are high above the earth, so great is His mercy toward those who fear Him; as far as the east is from the west, so far has He removed our transgressions from us. As a father pities his children, so the Lord pities those who fear Him. For He knows our frame; He remembers that we are dust. . . .

But the mercy of the Lord is from everlasting to everlasting on those who fear Him and His righteousness to children's children, to such as keep His covenant, and to those who remember His commandments to do them—Psalm 103:1-18, NKJV.

In his living room that evening, flanked by expensive brass vases and extravagant furniture, Munshi paced back and forth on his Persian rug, reading and re-reading the passage. "Thank You,

God, for saving me—for taking away my sins," he prayed. "Thank You for having pity on me."

The executive held the Bible to his chest between his folded arms and let tears flow unrestrained.

Genuine Conversion

A few days later, the apartment doorman escorted Mark up the elevator to Munshi's floor in hopes of acquiring a sizable tip.

"This is Mr. Biswas' floor, apartment number 1076." Mark handed the uniformed cicerone a one-rupee note for his trouble as the elevator door started to close.

Munshi bowed to his visitor like a servant to his master. "Thank you for coming. Please sit down."

Mark said, "It's an honor. This is a beautiful apartment."

"Thank you."

Did you have a chance to read Psalm 103?" Mark asked.

"Yes, sir. Many times. I am convinced I am a Christian. There is no doubt."

Mark's smiling cheeks lifted his glasses from the bridge of his nose. "God is good. Isn't He good, Munshi?"

"Yes, Pastor Buntain, He is."

"I've prayed for you every day," Mark wept. "God loves you so much."

"I know He does. I've been an evil person most of my life, but Jesus still died for me. After talking with you and reading from the Bible I could feel that God was with me. I knew He was real."

Mark wiped his eyes with his handkerchief. "I am so happy for you. Do you have any other questions?"

"Just one for now, Pastor." Mark leaned forward, expecting to hear an incisive theological question. "This has been troubling me for several days."

"Sure, what is it?"

Munshi's eyes showed concern. "What does Jesus have to do with a fetter?"

Mark chuckled as he reached for the Bible on the coffee table to explain.

CHAPTER TEN

Ramu

Ramu's brother and his fifteen-year-old bride knelt before the priest and the large statue of a goddess. Friends and family wept with joy as the priest, garbed in his Eastern robe, dabbed the couple's foreheads with water from the Ganges River. "This will add a special blessing to your marriage," he said.

The clay floor was littered with mango peelings and bouquets. Guests kept their plates and glasses full to be certain they would not offend the bride's father. Neighborhood children climbed the fence surrounding the yard just to get a whiff of the intoxicating scent of jasmine, tea leaves, curry, wine, incense, and rice.

Ramu was seventeen. He knew his marriage, just like his older brother's, would be arranged by his family. He hoped their selection would be a soft, bronze-skinned girl with a pear-shaped face, long lashes, and scintillating eyes that were framed by satiny hair.

Ramu's sister pointed toward the ceremony. "That will be you in a few years."

The boy grinned. "I hope my wife will be beautiful."

"That is for the family to decide," she reminded him with a smile. Ramu suddenly realized that his wife could rival an Indian elephant.

Maybe, Ramu thought, I should begin visiting the temples like I did when I was a boy to be certain the gods do not condemn me to a life with an ugly woman!

Ramu's parents had separated when he was young, yielding his father much grief. Ramu knew the identical scenario could ruin his life, and the festivity of fine food, wine, and dance did little to ease the boy's fears.

Accepting a Dare

On a steamy summer day Ramu boarded the train to Calcutta to visit his grandmother, a kind, quiet, wrinkled woman. She awakened Ramu every morning by folding him to her breast. Ramu liked visiting her. He enjoyed hanging out on street corners with neighborhood teenagers, mocking old men as they lugged their rickshaws, and teasing young girls, especially those wearing Western blue jeans—a sure sign of status.

"Hey!" his bushy-haired friend, Mohan, called out to a passing female. "What's your name?"

The slender girl did not divert from her path. "Can't you hear? Come here!" he shouted to her back. The girl kept walking.

"She's not interested in you," Ramu laughed. "Try that one over there." Ramu pointed to a humped, elderly woman.

"She's yours," Mohan snickered. "Hey, Ramu, how come you don't have a girl?"

"I have other things on my mind."

"What other things?"

"Just other things."

"Are you more interested in boys?" Mohan teased.

Ramu shoved his friend's shoulder as if he were angry.

The remainder of the morning was uneventful. Ramu began throwing pebbles at a pipe protruding from the cracked cement road. One of his friends was trying to whistle a tune on an empty beer bottle. Mohan, the curly haired neighbor, focused his attention on a trio of girls walking down the opposite side of the street. The girl in the middle was wearing a shapely pink saree, its multi-colored sequins sparkling in the sun.

"Ramu, if you're really a man, you'll ask one of those girls over there to go out," Mohan challenged.

Ramu studied the girls. "Nice . . . I like the one in the middle. But she probably has a boyfriend."

"Ask her anyway. I'll buy you two beers and take you to a movie if you do," added Mohan.

Ramu wondered if Mohan had enough money to fulfill his promise. His mouth watered thinking of the beers and an evening at the cinema.

"You promise?" Ramu asked.

"Yes," Mohan assured.

Ramu's First Love

The boys tracked the attractive trio to a ground floor apartment. Ramu began wishing he hadn't been tempted by Mohan's offer. Finally, his vocal antics caught the maidens' attention. Two of the girls swung around toward the boys while the other disappeared into the apartment. Ramu delicately explained that he wanted to go out with their sister, the girl who had slipped inside.

Minutes later, the chosen one emerged. "Did you want to see me?" she asked.

Ramu blinked a few times and stuck his hands in his back pockets. "My name is Ramu."

"I'm Asha."

"Hello," he said, shuffling his feet. "I was wondering if you would like to go out tonight to a movie?"

"I can't. My parents won't let me stay out late."

"What about tomorrow?"

"I go to Sunday school and church."

"How about after church?"

"I guess that would be all right. It's over at noon. I'll just tell my parents I'm going somewhere with a girlfriend."

The two of them smiled at each other awkwardly. Ramu blushed as he nodded goodbye.

The following afternoon the two teenagers had difficulty keeping their minds on the movie. The dark hall was a perfect place for Ramu to stroke the girl's delicate hand. Her sudden jolt did not dissuade Ramu. He lodged his left arm around her shoulder, his eyes fixed on the screen. Asha leaned her head against his shoulder like a purring kitten.

They walked home hand-in-hand. "I don't know what love is," the boy said, "but I think I've fallen in love with you." Asha giggled. "I'm serious," he said. "Will you marry me?"

"You're funny," she laughed softly.

Ramu wanted to show how much he cared for her, but he knew it would only make his departure for home more difficult. Dejectedly, the teenager watched Asha slide back into her cubbyhole.

Heartsick With Love

The sunshine was glaring off the bumpers of passing cars later that afternoon as the young man stationed himself on a familiar doorstep.

"Look, it's Ramu, the man with all the girls." Mohan scuffled up to his friend. "How was it?"

"She was nice. I really liked her."

"How was the movie?"

"Fine." Ramu's jaw drooped.

Mohan became more somber. He could tell Ramu was preoccupied with something other than the movie. "What are you going to do?" the friend asked. "You're leaving tomorrow."

"I don't know. If only I were older, then I could stay."

"Stay!" Mohan urged.

"My family wouldn't approve."

"You're seventeen. You're old enough to do what you want."

"My family must arrange my marriage."

Mohan surrendered the debate and lit up a cigarette. "My friend, you're missing out on a good thing. She's a beauty."

Ramu glared at his friend as if to say, Thanks, that's all I need to hear right now.

Ramu felt as though his heart were being stretched from Calcutta to his homeland as his train steamed northward. Ramu mourned his departure. Asha held his heart in her palm, and the separation threatened to rob him of any chance he had for happiness.

Gazing out the window of his compartment, Ramu was oblivious to a herd of rampaging goats and the waving hands of village children. With each railroad tie the train thundered over, Ramu knew he was streaking further and further away from his first love. And nothing else mattered.

Making Tough Choices

The young man's poetic letters helped the relationship survive until the following summer when Ramu ran away to Calcutta. Shortly thereafter, the young lovers were married in a private ceremony. Ramu's family refused to attend the wedding because their son had betrayed their wishes. His letters to them were returned unopened, his pleas for clemency unnoticed.

"This girl does not belong to our family," his father insisted when Ramu and his new bride returned to his homeland unannounced. Even his brothers and sisters refused to invite the newlyweds into their hovels. "You are not welcome here. You have embarrassed us," one brother said.

Asha could see Ramu's fists clench and the vessels in his neck bulge. "No, Ramu," she whispered in his ear. "Let's go back to Calcutta. This will not solve anything." Ramu was motionless as he weighed her words. "Let's go, Ramu. He's your brother. Give him time."

Mechanical difficulties and delays made the rail ride back to Calcutta more tiresome than usual.

For many miles, Ramu chronicled in his mind his happy experiences with his family, regretting that his decision to marry had severed him from those he loved. Asha could read his mind like a journal, squeezing his arm with every new page. A disheartened Ramu wondered if his family would ever restore him as their son.

"Someday they will accept us," Asha said, leaning her head against his shoulder just as she had on their first meeting.

Ramu wished he could be so sure.

The Musical

Asha's parents expected their daughter to continue attending the church in which she had grown up, pastored by Mark Buntain.

Ramu, however, perceived the Christian church as just another obstacle between Asha and his family.

"Asha, I don't want you to go," he said emphatically. "If my family hears that you attend a Christian church, they will never accept you."

"Ramu, tonight is special. The choir is performing a musical. Please let me go. My family wants me to come. Please," she begged.

He could hear the desperation in her voice. Still he refused to let his authority be questioned. "I said no. You must stay home."

"Please," she pleaded. "Just this service. Please, Ramu."

Ramu took a deep breath and thought. "If you promise this will be your last, you can go."

"That will be my promise if you come with me," Asha bargained.

Ramu's initial anger from his wife's proposition mellowed into a slice of admiration for her shrewdness. He paused, then said, "I will come, but just because I don't want you to keep asking."

The musical ended with the audience standing to sing, "Oh come let us adore Him, Oh come let us adore Him . . ." Ramu stayed glued to his seat during the first stanza before Asha pulled him up beside her. Ramu knew he could never admit to his wife how much he was enjoying the service. That would merely provoke her to keep begging him to come.

"Hello, Asha," a man called from the center of the sanctuary after the church service. She waved at the Caucasian as he charged through the traffic. "This must be your husband." He offered his hand.

"Yes," Ramu said, accepting the handshake.

"I'm Pastor Buntain. I'm sorry I didn't acknowledge you from the pulpit. Asha's mother just told me who you were. Please accept my apologies."

Ramu thought it was peculiar that a minister would want to greet him from the stage in front of so many people.

Mark was still shaking Ramu's hand when he asked, "Will you and Asha come to my office tomorrow afternoon?"

The white man's eyes were blurred by his thick glasses, so Ramu could not determine if the priest was angry with them or if he was just trying to convert them.

Ramu cleared his throat. "I must work tomorrow."

"Then come after work," Mark said.

The couple looked at each other, hoping they could concoct a legitimate excuse. Neither spoke.

"Then I'll be waiting for you," Mark waved.

Ramu was fearful of this man. If only he could have read his eyes. Asha was afraid the meeting would make Ramu even more hostile toward Christianity.

An Invitation to Return

As the husband and wife approached Mark's office the next day, Ramu whispered, "Maybe he won't be here. Maybe he's been called from his office."

Mark opened the door after the second knock. "Come in," he said as he hugged both visitors.

Ramu was startled by the friendly reception. After all, he had just met this priest yesterday. The white man with the graying hair looked at Asha, then at Ramu. "I love you because God loves you."

"Thank you," said Asha.

Ramu dismissed formalities. "I am not a Christian. I do not believe as you."

"I know," Mark said. "But will you give me a few moments to read from God's Word?"

Ramu shifted his eyes from his hands to Mark. "Yes, if you wish." As the preacher began flipping through his well-worn Bible, Ramu examined the countless books on the shelves beside him and the photographs residing on the blue-gray walls.

The young man paid little attention to the complicated scriptures. "I'm confused," he said every five minutes. "This is so foreign to me."

"Then you must come to the services on Sunday so you can understand this."

Ramu thought, This man is as cunning as my wife.

Asha pulled her two hundred pound husband to the third row of the sanctuary that Sunday. They vaulted over a family of four to two chairs in the middle of the row.

"Why do we have to be so close?" Ramu asked.

"You promised Pastor you would come."

"Yes, but I never said I'd sit in the front."

"This way he'll know you're here."

All eyes seemed to focus on the Caucasian priest in the white shirt. Ramu enjoyed the music, the choir, and the enthusiasm in the sanctuary. The audience went from a roar to a hush as Mark made his way to the pulpit. Ramu's face tingled as the pastor prayed for God's presence.

Then, Mark said, "It's my pleasure to introduce to you a young man who has become very special to me." Ramu squirmed as the preacher stared in his direction. "I would like Ramu Rao to stand." The young man's body uncoiled. Mark's hands were still clapping when Ramu sat down. "If you have not met Ramu, please greet him this morning or after service this evening."

Ramu had no intention of attending the evening meeting. But he could not disappoint this preacher who had recognized him in such an esteemed manner. By six o'clock that evening, the couple was again seated in the third row.

Ramu's New Allegiance

Ramu felt like he was in front of a firing squad and Mark Buntain was firing holy bullets. At the close of his message the tall preacher summoned those who wanted to receive Jesus Christ to come to the altar. Ramu unsuccessfully tried to tie himself to his chair, for, within seconds, his body was compelled to approach the altar. When he opened his eyes, the pastor was standing over him, his hands clasped together, his head raised to the heavens.

The church became empty, save the two men and Asha praying at her seat. It was nearly ten o'clock when the two men rose to their feet. Ramu had received Christ as his Lord and Savior.

From the church steps, in a brisk breeze, Mark watched the couple walk home down Royd Street. He pivoted his eyes toward the moon and conversed with his Creator. "Thank You, God. Thank You, God. Thank You, Jesus."

Ramu wrote to his family to confess his new allegiance to Jesus Christ. If they opened his letter, he knew it would anger them. "But they must know so one day they can receive Christ as well," he explained to Asha.

His father responded promptly in writing: "To us you are as good as dead. Do not write or return again. We no longer know you."

Ramu wept as he read those words. Asha, from behind, put her chin on her husband's head.

"Don't worry," she said. "One day they will understand."

Shocking Betrayal

Years later, while Ramu was working, he asked a subordinate to retrieve a report he had forgotten at home. The worker returned from Ramu's house with distressing news. "Your wife's mother said Asha took your baby to the hospital."

Ramu dropped the clipboard in his hand and sped out the gate in a company vehicle. Asha was not at the hospital; she had never arrived. Ramu drove frantically from street to street, from neighbor to neighbor, and through the bazaar, trying to locate his wife and baby. Friends joined the hunt.

After several hours of searching, word reached Ramu that Asha had been seen with a boy across town.

"What did the boy look like?" Ramu asked angrily.

"He was about 5'10", about nineteen, with his hair parted down the middle. That's about all I could see," the friend said.

Ramu gritted his teeth. "It must be Prasad," he growled. "A friend of Asha's family."

Ramu suspected that Prasad was interfering with his marriage, but he had no proof. He ran the white two-door sedan into the curb in front of their basement apartment.

To his surprise, Asha was sitting on the floor with their child.

"Where have you been?" he barked.

"The hospital. The baby had a check-up."

"I went to the hospital," he stared.

"You did? Why?"

"Your mother forgot to tell my friend it was a check-up. I thought something was wrong with the baby, so I drove to the hospital."

Asha could feel her face becoming flushed. She turned, hoping Ramu wouldn't notice. "You must have gotten there too late."

"I don't think so. You didn't go to the hospital, did you?"

The young woman searched her husband's eyes for a hint that he knew where she had been. She started to give him another explanation.

"The doctor was busy, so . . ."

"No, tell me the truth."

"All right," she sighed. "I was with a friend."

"Was it Prasad?"

Asha, astonished by his discovery, swallowed. "Yes, I was with Prasad."

"Why? What were you doing?" Ramu yelled, slamming the door closed.

"We . . . just talked."

"Is that all?" he snapped.

"Yes."

"What else?"

"Nothing. Why are you so upset?" she said, frowning.

"What else did you do with Prasad?"

"I don't know."

"You better know." Ramu threw a clay cup to the cement floor, particles scattering around Asha's feet. He awaited an answer. She gave none. "Tell me what you were doing."

She hesitated. "We were going to run away together, but I got scared."

Revenge or Reconciliation?

The shocking admission hit Ramu like a bucket of cold water. He paused and then bolted out of her sight. Minutes later he was waiting outside Prasad's house, plotting to take "the thief's" life. Ramu's hands were nearly tearing the steering wheel off. "He must die. He has taken my wife from me. I'm going to kill him!" he yelled to an empty car.

Suddenly a verse flashed into his mind: "Thou shalt not kill." Ramu tried to ignore it, to rid it from his conscience, but it was to no avail. The distraught husband turned the key and drove aimlessly through the streets. The white compact turned sharply into the church parking area and forged through a large, swamp-like puddle.

Mark heard the brakes screech outside his office and bounded to the door to investigate. "What is it, Ramu?" He could see the boy's eyes were swollen from tears.

"Asha was leaving me."

The pastor looked bewildered. "Why?"

"To go off with another boy."

Mark closed his eyes quickly to hide his own disappointment. "Hop in," he gestured to his car. "We'll take care of this. Where is she?"

There was no time to find a driver. So for one of the few times since his arrival in Calcutta, Mark was driving through the city's obstacle course with reckless abandon. The streets were rapid streams with objects riding the currents helplessly. He knew Ramu's fledgling relationship with God was weighing in the balance. The stampeding vehicles about him were the least of Mark's concerns.

"Dear God, help me to say the right thing," he said to himself as Ramu wept in the passenger's seat. "These are Your children. Bring them back together."

The young woman was noticeably disturbed, embarrassed by Mark's entrance. Yet, six hours later, the couple was hugging and asking forgiveness from each other. They didn't even notice that Mark had departed. The preacher was already cautiously creeping down the road, smiling, with both hands fastened securely to the steering wheel.

"Thank You, Lord," Mark yelled out his window.

Confronting Another Crisis

The luminous moon was shielded by the curtains in Mark's office. Only an air conditioner given to him by a generous American made work bearable, even at night. His carrot-sized fingers were sliding down his daily calendar, which looked like a grocery list, when the phone rang.

"Yes?" Mark answered the third signal. Seconds later he stood up from his desk. "Where is he? Oh God! I'll be there in a few minutes," Mark said. The pastor hurried down the steps into his car.

"To Ramu's house, and hurry, man," he blurted to the driver.

The driver could sense the panic in Mark's voice. From the back seat the minister prayed, unaware that the driver was deliberately disobeying what few traffic laws there were in Calcutta. The vehicle arrived at their destination unscathed, and the driver with the brown beret wheeled around to awaken his passenger from his prayer.

"Good work, man," Mark said. "Wait on me, will you?" The driver raised his hand and bent his head sideways.

"Ramu, friend, what has happened?" Ramu was sitting on a stool, staring into his folded hands. Mark was unsure if the neighbors were encircling the new Christian to restrain him or just to comfort him.

"Ramu," he repeated, walking closer. Ramu didn't budge. "Ramu, look at me, friend." The face that arose was wrought with hate. "What has happened? Tell me," Mark peered down. Ramu looked away. "How can I help you if you . . ."

"She was with that boy again," Ramu interrupted loudly. His head tilted forward into his hands.

Mark's voice softened. "I came because they said you tried to kill someone. Was it the boy?"

Ramu nodded his head and burst into tears. "I'm sorry, Pastor."

Mark pressed his hand into Ramu's back. "I know you are," he said.

"When I heard she was with him, I couldn't control myself. I swung a machete and nearly hit him."

"It's over, son. God knows you're sorry."

Mark left his sobbing friend momentarily and joined the neighbors in the next room. The neighbors explained how it took all three of them to drag Ramu out of the boy's house, but not before his brandishing blade sliced into a table top and a couch.

"Where's Asha?" Mark asked.

"I don't know," Ramu said, gritting his teeth.

"We're going to find her. Where is she?"

"I don't want to see her. She tried to come back, but I wouldn't let her in the house. She pounded and pounded on the door, but I just didn't want to see her face. How could she do this, Pastor?"

"Where should we look?" the preacher repeated.

"You might find her at Hansi's."

"Let's go, Ramu."

The tall Indian stared at Mark, resisting the temptation to yell at his most beloved friend.

Ramu said, "I can't. It doesn't matter anymore. I'm going home to my parents."

Mark's rebuttals were ignored.

The tall minister knew he had to act quickly. The following morning Mark returned to his office and canceled all his appointments. His secretary knew that meant no interruptions; her employer needed to be alone with God.

That afternoon Mark arrived at Ramu's house to take him for a ride.

"Where are we going?" the young man asked.

"We're going to find Asha."

"No, we're not! I told you, I don't want to see her!"

"Get in!" Mark demanded. This time Ramu obeyed.

Mark drove without a word, eventually parking the vehicle in a secluded alley.

"Ramu, I know you still love Asha."

"Pastor, I'm not sure anymore."

"I am, Ramu; she's your wife. God gave her to you. He wants to bring you back together."

"She lied to me. She betrayed me."

"I know she has, but you must forgive her."

"I can't. You don't understand. She ran off with another boy. How can I ever touch her again?"

Without responding, Mark broke into prayer. Two hours later, two teary-eyed men made their way up a rickety stairway to the third floor of an old tenant house where Asha was staying.

"Is Asha here?" Mark asked a woman at the door.

"No," she said nervously.

"Ma'am, I asked you a question," Mark glared.

"No."

"Is Asha here?" he repeated firmly.

"Yes," she pointed to the door behind her. "In there."

Ramu waited outside while Mark proceeded toward the bedroom door. Asha didn't react to Mark's arrival. Her petite body lay across the bed, face down.

"Get up," Mark ordered. Asha was reluctant. "Get up. I'm not leaving until you do."

Asha rolled over. "Why should I?"

"Ramu is here waiting for you."

Her eyes grew. "Pastor, he'll hurt me."

"No, Asha, come with me. He wants to talk."

Within minutes, Asha and Ramu were riding speechlessly, side by side, in the back seat of Mark's car en route to the couple's apartment. It was like an uncomfortable blind date: neither could look at the other. The trio, once inside, sat on the floor like children in a sandbox. Ramu stared at the floor. Asha stared at Mark.

"Asha, do you promise you'll never do this again?" Mark asked.

"I promise," she said softly. "I just . . ."

"Are you sorry about what you did?"

"Yes."

"Ramu, Asha says she wants your forgiveness."

"I can't. I can't," he said, peering at the dusty floor.

"Jesus has forgiven her. You must, too. I don't understand why this has happened," Mark said, "but I know it's God's will that you two are together. I can't see you separated. If I fail to get you back together, I don't know where my ministry will be."

Ramu looked up sharply, aware that Mark felt personally responsible.

"God," Mark prayed with his eyes open, "thank You for binding together Ramu and Asha. They love You and each other. Help them to forgive one another as You have forgiven them." As he prayed, the minister opened his eyes and placed Asha's arm around Ramu's shoulder. He could see Ramu trying to wink back tears. The prayer ended and Asha leaped into her husband's arms, hugging him earnestly.

"I'm sorry. I do love you. Please forgive me. I promise I will never do this again," Asha cried. "I won't . . ."

Before she could complete her phrase, Ramu had drawn her into his burly arms and caressed her back.

"I know. I love you, too. Everything is going to work this time. I just know it," Ramu declared.

"I forgive you, Asha. I love you."

Suddenly, the door to the apartment closed. Mark had retreated to his automobile so the couple could be alone and he could be alone with God.

Moments later, children in the streets were pointing at the white man who was visibly crying and talking to himself in his parked car with his eyes closed.

CHAPTER ELEVEN

Sharma

Black geldings pranced in rows of three past Buckingham Palace, their saddles and reins ornamented with chrome buckles and buttons. Their flowing tails and finely groomed manes bounced as their riders saluted Queen Elizabeth. The British soldiers, wearing their customary headdress, leather boots, and red coats, raised their sparkling swords in perpendicular fashion.

Young boys and girls jostled one another to get a clearer view of their queen. Her white gown was adorned with lace trim and precious sequins. The diamond studded necklace complemented her crown, which rose above her wavy brown hair. Youngsters marveled at her gold throne and the intricate designs in the tall backrest.

Television cameras, announcers, and reporters were scattered along the sidewalk, broadcasting the event to the world. Sharma, a young reporter from Calcutta, had been with Radio India for several years when her superiors selected her for the assignment, an opportunity every journalist envied. Colleagues rumored she was chosen because of her attractive looks and family name. It was not uncommon for Sharma to be mistaken for a model or movie star. "No, no," she would insist, blushing. "I'm just a radio person."

She did have the appearance of a cover girl: a trim figure, high cheekbones, extra-long lashes, and crimson lips. But her wealthy parents never would have tolerated a modeling career for their daughter. After all, they were personal friends of the Prime Minister, among other high-ranking officials. Sharma's father, an officer in the military, had been awarded the Medal of Service by the King of England. Her family had a reputation, an image to preserve. Even Sharma's radio career had been a disappointment to her father.

After Sharma's first child was born, she managed to please both her father and husband by forfeiting her promising career. It wasn't necessary for her to earn money. Her husband, the son of a wealthy judge, made a comfortable income through his textile business. She could stay at home and involve herself in civic affairs.

Sharma had grown up praying each morning and night to her gods, a ritual she carried into adulthood. She wore only white, a sign of righteousness before the spirits. Each day, after her mid-morning tea, the servants were ordered from the living room. For fifteen minutes Sharma demanded silence as she meditated on the goodness of the gods.

Her two unmarried daughters, on the other hand, were unsympathetic to their mother's devout worship, dismissing it as traditional nonsense. Periodically, Sharma would hear them laughing at her through their bedroom doors. Their disbelief troubled Sharma so that she prayed to her gods daily to preserve their souls.

A Joyous Reunion

One hot Sunday, three attractive girls wearing designer jeans and imported blouses slid into the back row of Mark Buntain's church. Following the inspiring message, Sharma's two girls glided to the prayer room. The tallest girl remained in her seat. Mark slipped to the back of the auditorium as the song leader led in another chorus.

"Would you like to give your heart to Jesus?" Mark asked the girl. "If you'll come, I'll pray with you."

Mark silently pleaded for her soul as he awaited her response. "Yes, I'll come," she said.

After Mark had prayed with the girl at the altar, she lifted her head. "Do you know who I am?"

"I'm sorry, I don't."

"I'm Pyari."

Mark leaped to his feet. "You're Pyari? I can't believe it!" he shouted to a nearly empty prayer room. "Where have you been?"

"I've been away at school," she smiled proudly.

Mark remembered when he first met Pyari. She must have been only five or six years old. After school she walked three blocks to play with Bonnie, Mark's daughter.

Then, from the Buntain's flat, the young girl often skipped to a nightclub where her mother worked as a dancer. Standing on a drum outside the bar, she had watched men make passes at her mother. Mark had lost contact with the frightened child when she left Calcutta with her mother some years earlier.

Mark was busy introducing Pyari to several parishioners when a motorcycle suddenly roared through the church gate. A staff member was talking to the driver when Mark interrupted.

"It's so wonderful!" he exclaimed. "The tall girl over there gave her heart to God tonight."

The stranger seated on the bike snapped angrily. "Oh, she did? Well, that's my wife."

The young man, Kamdesh, echoed a command across the parking lot. "Pyari!" The girl turned with an alarmed expression on her face. Then, almost as if she were being forced at gunpoint, she boarded the bike.

Upon further investigation, Mark discovered the couple had been separated for some time. Both drank heavily and attended ungodly parties. Pyari's modeling career was blossoming, and her agent was negotiating a lucrative movie contract.

As evidence of their sinful lifestyle mounted, Mark became concerned for their souls. He often closed the door to his office and turned out the lights. In the blackness, Mark sought the face of God for these two young people. The preacher would pray until his voice was drained and fast for days, hoping they would respond to the Holy Spirit.

An Unexpected Visitor

The morning sun was half exposed when Mark lumbered up the concrete steps to his simple office. Beads of moisture already were accumulating around his collar. A resounding knock at his door caused him to flinch.

Surprisingly, Pyari's husband dropped into the vinyl chair in front of Mark's desk. The preacher could see Kamdesh's tough exterior melting into tear drops. "Even if I don't get my wife back, I want to be right with God," he confided.

Mark inspected the man's eyes for any sign of insincerity. "Maybe you can have God . . . and have your wife back," he said.

Kamdesh sat up. "How? She won't even talk to me."

"There's one thing I know, son: All things are possible for God."

Two days later, Mark orchestrated a dinner meeting with Pyari and Kamdesh at one of Calcutta's finest hotels. But with midnight approaching they left the restaurant in separate taxis, unable to resolve their differences.

Mark's faith was not deflated, and he encouraged Kamdesh to continue praying. "God can perform a miracle," Mark told his young friend.

Refusing to Give Up

On his way home for lunch one day, Mark cruised by his own apartment on Camac Street. The guard at the entrance to the Buntain's flat scratched his head as the preacher passed without stopping. Mark had suddenly felt God was prompting him to find Pyari, and now. He traced her to Sharma's house, a three-story building with separate apartments on each floor. With the front door ajar, Mark called out for Pyari.

"What are you doing here?" the model fumed.

"Pyari, will you please understand that God loves you? I don't want to bother you. It's the Holy Spirit. He wants you to accept Him. God loves you in spite of your sin."

"Leave me alone. Just leave me alone. I'm not interested," she whimpered.

Mark eventually left, shaking his head, momentarily discouraged by her rejection of Christ. Hours later, however, the preacher returned for another attempt.

"Hello, ma'am, my name is Pastor Mark Buntain. Is Pyari here?"

Sharma stared at the visitor. "She is not."

"Are Padmini or Shakuntala here?" Mark asked, wishing to speak to the two girls who had accompanied Pyari to his church weeks earlier.

"Yes, they're my daughters."

"May I come in and speak with them?" The woman drew the door back cautiously.

"Wait here. I'll get them," Sharma said sternly. From the other room Mark could hear the woman interrogating her young daughters. "Why has he come here?"

"I don't know," he heard a voice say.

The woman led one of her daughters into the modern living room.

"Hello, Shakuntala. I came to see Pyari, but while I was here I wanted to confirm that you will be taking water baptism on Sunday," Mark said.

Sharma recaptured the teacup that nearly slipped from her hand. "Why didn't I know about this?" the mother asked scornfully.

Mark rose to leave before an argument could erupt. Sharma patted her gray hair and led Mark to the elevator.

Mark stopped. "You know, Mrs. Das, Jesus loves you."

The woman's sagging frame straightened. "We believe in the same Jesus you do," she said.

"No, Mrs. Das, you don't. We believe Jesus is the Son of God who died for our sins." The elevator door opened, and Mark bowed farewell. Annoyed by his parting comment, Sharma stood still for a moment, then began analyzing Mark's description of Jesus.

Healer and Savior

Sometime later, Sharma's husband contracted a high fever. He refused to go to the hospital, and Sharma could see his health was deteriorating. She ran to the feet of her carved idols and prayed. After hearing of his sickness, Mark sent two women to pray for the gentleman.

At first Sharma was reluctant, but she finally conceded to let them enter her house. The two women placed their hands on her husband's arm and lowered their heads. Sharma watched carefully.

How peculiar, she thought. These women are crying for a man they do not know. Suddenly, for fear that she would invoke the gods' wrath,

Sharma hastily rushed the women from the room. "The gods are angry. They will punish us for having these women in our house," she said, almost loud enough to be heard.

When the commotion had ceased, Sharma laid beside her sick husband and prayed herself to sleep. But later, seemingly without provocation, Sharma sat up against the headboard and began making strange noises.

Her startled husband rasped, "What's wrong?"

"Who was that looking at me?"

"There's no one here," he whispered, relieved. "You were having a dream."

"There was! It was a man. I think it was Jesus."

Her husband, still burning with fever, moaned, "It was a dream; go back to sleep." Hours later, however, when Mr. Das awakened, he was completely cured of his illness.

Sharma was convinced Jesus had come to her home and healed her husband.

The following Sunday, Sharma sat with her daughters in the middle of the sanctuary and cried. Tears channeled into the wrinkles in her face and were still there the next morning. Sharma dressed in an attractive pink saree and walked into Mark's office.

"Pastor, I am wearing colored clothing for the first time. I have decided to pray to Christ. I am free. I have come to tell you that I now believe that

Jesus Christ is alive and I have accepted Him as my Savior." Then she asked, "What should I do with my statues?"

Mark replied, "Mrs. Das, you know what you must do with them."

That evening Sharma began lifting the images from her shelves. And the moment she disposed of them, a peace flooded her mind. She finally knew the joy that can only come through pleasing Christ.

Rejoicing, Remorse, and Remembrance

Days passed. Mark had resolved that at least Sharma had come to God as a result of his quest to reunite Pyari and Kamdesh. Yet his prayers persisted for the young couple. He realized he had done everything *humanly* possible. One evening, as Mark rose to leave his office, the couple entered hand-in-hand. Mark was stunned.

"We wanted you to know we have gotten back together," Pyari said.

"Congratulations!" Mark exclaimed, his cheeks swollen with joy. Months earlier he had dreamed of conducting a special wedding so Pyari and Kamdesh could renew their vows, but the opportunity had never materialized.

"As my gift to you," he now said eagerly, "will you let me give you a Christian wedding—a celebration?"

Pyari and Kamdesh looked at one another, smiled, and nodded their approval.

Mark went to great lengths to display his affection for the couple. The sanctuary resembled the setting of a royal wedding with flowers strewn across the altars and large candelabras rising from the platform. The church youth choir sang like an assembly of angels as Mark prayed silently over the young lovers.

Mark had rented a suite at the hotel for them and ordered that a dozen roses be placed on Pyari's pillow. Pyari sat on the bed with tears in her eyes.

"Why are you crying?" Kamdesh asked.

"I'm just happy. I now know what love is."

Kamdesh knew exactly what she was alluding to. The couple embraced, flattening a rose or two. But Mark wouldn't have cared. That evening Mark's head rested comfortably on *his* pillow for the first time in months.

In the next year and a half, Pyari and Kamdesh participated in a missionary training program in a distant city. Mark wrote to them often, and the couple reciprocated with letters to him.

One letter from Kamdesh, however, stole Mark's breath:

Dear Mark:

I regret to inform you that Pyari and I have divorced. We are grateful for all

you've done. You've shown us the love
of Jesus. I can never turn away from Him
because of that.

Unfortunately, Pyari has chosen to
return to her old ways. It hurts me to
write you this, but I thought you should
know. We each love you . . .

The preacher removed his glasses. His face fell
into his arms on the desk. "Oh, God," he cried.
"Oh, God." His eyes were already red. His handkerchief could not catch the tears fast enough.
Leaning back in his chair, Mark stared at the letter. He read it again and again. The handkerchief
was drenched. He wiped his tears away with the
back of his hand and sat, expressionless and numb.

Noticing a small brass paperweight on the corner of his desk, Mark tossed it in the air and caught
it. A surprisingly peaceful look came to his face
as he studied the small, brass token—a gift from
one of his most faithful parishioners: Sharma. In
time perhaps Pyari—like Sharma—would put her
old ways behind her and give herself to Jesus, Mark
thought. For now, he could only wait and pray.

CHAPTER TWELVE

Premdas

His muscular chest strained the buttons on his plaid shirt, making the top two unlatchable. His arms bowed out from his shoulders. His wide neck and scowling face made him look like a bulldog. Straight, shoulder-length hair was parted to one side. He wore a thin, black mustache and an earring in his left ear.

Children in the neighborhood said Premdas' lips were red from drinking blood. They told stories of how he had broken a man's neck with his bare hands and another's back. Regardless of the rumors, the knife strapped to his right thigh was enough to scare most spectators. As he and his comrades strutted down the street of their village, one by one doors closed, and children were pulled into their hovels.

The young terrorist frightened even his own parents. His father, a respectable businessman, had married a devout Christian woman after Premdas' mother died. Although Telesseri was Premdas' stepmother, she loved him and his two sisters as her own. While they were growing up, she had taken them to Sunday school and read them the Scriptures each morning. But once Premdas entered high school, he spent his Sundays weight lifting with a group of older boys. Without the influence of the church, the Bible in his room became just another decoration.

An Enticing Proposition

By the hour, he drilled with the iron bars in a makeshift gym. The other boys admired Premdas' dedication and strength. His build equaled that of a grown man!

"Premdas!" a voice called. Two older boys overshadowed Premdas as he positioned himself beneath a bar. "We have some ganja. You want some? We're gettin' outta here."

"No, I don't smoke," the weight lifter replied, breathing deeply, preparing for another set of repetitions.

"What do ya mean? Have ya tried it?"

"No, it's not good for weight lifting."

The boys shook their heads. "Man, what da you do for fun, lift weights?" teased a puny boy with matted eyebrows.

"I guess," Premdas grimaced as he hoisted the bar again. "Well, what do you guys do for fun, use drugs?"

"We're in a gang," the shorter boy spouted. The other boy looked around to see if anyone heard his zealous companion's remark.

"A gang? Why join a gang?" Premdas asked as he sat up.

"This society is oppressive. We're at war to change things." Premdas listened intently. "Our purpose is to bring this society down so another that'll help the people and give us respect in the world can take its place."

"I have nothing against the people around me and our country."

"It's society's fault everyone don't have a job and food."

"That's not true," Premdas protested. "Every country has its poor, even America and Russia."

"Their problems are much less than ours," the rebel challenged, "but that's because they're the cause of the world's problems."

"You can't blame them for everything."

"Yes, but we have to tear down a world system that profits only the superpowers."

Premdas thought for a moment. "I just don't think you can blame society or the system for all our troubles."

"You've been listening to too many lies," the boy fumed. "If you really want to help the poor, you'll join our gang."

Finding a Cause

The rhetoric was enough to pique Premdas' curiosity and convince him to meet the gang's leader. The three boys weaved through a series of alleys near the Hooghly River and into the rear entrance of an abandoned store. The large Indian at the door threw Premdas against the brick wall and scavenged his body for weapons then trailed the boys down a flight of stairs into a black hole. A few members were playing cards under a hanging bulb in the soggy basement. A young man was swinging a machete across the room like a shadow-boxing prize-fighter.

"Who is this?" snapped a tall man in his mid-twenties.

"This is Premdas. He's interested in joining the gang," the small friend informed.

The leader seemed impressed by Premdas' physique. "A weight lifter?" he asked, picking at his scabbed fist.

"Yes," Premdas said.

"Why do you want to join our gang?"

Premdas wasn't sure he wanted to join, but he knew he could be beaten severely if he refused. "I don't like the things around us and all the poverty," he said.

"Do you hate it enough to fight?" the leader asked.

Premdas stammered. "If there's no other way."

"For us there is no other way. When we say fight, you fight," he yelled, slamming his fist down on the table. "Otherwise we have no use for you."

Premdas was trembling.

"Are you ready to die, to give your life?" the Indian snapped.

"If it was necessary," he answered.

The leader was expressionless. "Be here tomorrow at four, and if you tell anyone about this place, you'll be sorry."

The seventeen-year-old was grateful to escape the fortress, yet he knew he had to return. Otherwise, his family might find him floating in the Hooghly.

Gang Wars

The guard frisked Premdas again the following afternoon, this time with less hostility. About twelve members, ranging from thirteen to thirty in age, congregated in the basement. Premdas stood on his tiptoes. A brown sheet was covering something on the large table in front of Suman, the leader.

"We have just received our knives," he said, yanking away the sheet to reveal the treasures.

The room bubbled with chatter as Suman distributed the utensils to the gang members. Premdas was handed a six inch blade. Mimicking the others, he stuffed the knife into his pants. The room was suddenly quiet as the leader stood on a riser to give his weekly discourse.

"We are making progress. We are winning!" He waited for the mob's cheers to end. "But we must continue fighting."

Premdas could feel his stomach shift as the gang roared its approval. Soon his voice joined in with his peers in chanting, "Victory, victory, victory!"

A week later, the gang was summoned to its headquarters with word to prepare for war. The night was mysteriously calm as the leader led the troop into a cemetery. Limestone shrines and Muslim gravestones made Premdas uncomfortable.

He bumped shoulders with fellow goondas* at the rear of the pack, a knife welded to his hand. He couldn't see the enemy over the taller boys. Then, without warning, the gangs converged. Premdas began swinging his "sword" violently, connecting only with air. The novice fighter soon found himself in a deluge of bodies.

Premdas' mind flashed to his parents, then his sisters. They thought he was down the road lifting weights. The knife fell to his side for a moment. An attacker missed his head with a vicious swipe. Premdas retaliated with a fist-blow

* *goondas:* gangsters

under the boy's rib cage. By now the police were approaching. Suman herded his gang, and the warriors fled down the street like wild dogs.

Back at the hideout, the gang was applauding its victory, but Premdas' joy vanished when he learned one of his friends had been severely injured.

The injury to his friend, however, did little to curb his violent cravings. Months passed, and Premdas' participation in the gang fights continued.

The thrill of rioting and fighting was stimulating. Premdas never had so much amusement. His respect for life was being smothered by a need to release the fury bridled in his fists.

Escalating Violence

Premdas' parents no longer knew their son. They feared him. They prayed for him daily, pleading with him to terminate his association with his "vicious" friends. They were unaware their son was rising in rank, becoming a leader in the gang. One night they locked his bedroom door, trying to keep him from taking his place as prince of the streets. He broke the door down; he had a ruthless mission to accomplish.

After drinking several beers, he and his friends captured a rival gang member. They pinned the

boy to the turf so Premdas could punch him bru-
tally. When it was over, the boys hovered over the
beaten body as if it were a trophy buck. The splat-
tering blood coated their hands and splotched
their clothes. And they didn't care.

They wanted more blood.

They hid outside a debtor's house. When the
man stepped onto the street, Premdas tackled him.
Gang members watched gleefully as the teenager
pounded the man's head into the cold cement. The
right side of the victim's face was swollen beyond
recognition. Fortunately, the lights of an approaching vehicle halted the beating. Premdas and his
buddies scurried behind a wall, then fled home.

Starting Over

Premdas' parents were waiting for him like an
unmerciful jury.

"They're going to put you in jail," Telesseri
cried. His father caressed her shivering shoulder.

Premdas didn't know what to say. "What are
you talking about?"

"You're my only son," his father said softly.
"Let's move to Calcutta and start over."

"Go ahead," Premdas defied. "I don't need to
run from anything. I didn't do anything."

"The police know you beat up a boy earlier
tonight. They were here. Do you want to go to jail?
Is that what you want?" his father yelled.

"No. I'm not going to jail."

"If you don't change your ways, that's where you're going to wind up. Even now it may be too late. The police will be back."

"Leave me alone. They're not going to put me in jail for punching someone in the face. Anyway, he deserved it."

"I don't know what happened. All I know is that we love you, son. And we need to move away from here, to Calcutta, and start over."

The thought of not having to avoid the police was becoming more appealing to the young man. After all, his father was right; the officers would keep coming back until they tracked him down.

Premdas was silent for a long time. "All right," he agreed finally, "let's go to Calcutta."

His father and mother wiped their tears and began preparing for their journey.

Are You Real, God?

In Calcutta, Premdas spent many days hibernating in his room, thinking. His hands were stained with memories. The ghosts of his victims seemed to seek revenge on his soul. At night he dreamed of a machete severing his arm or the barrel of a pistol pointing up his nose. He woke up every few hours, expecting to see that his fantasies were, in fact, reality. His blanket was wrapped around his perspiring body like a bulletproof shield. Dreams were so vivid that Premdas trembled in his sleep.

His stepmother was often awakened by his groaning. She would sit on his cot and brush the sweat from his forehead. "You must accept God," she'd say. "Premdas, you'll never be happy until you find Jesus."

He knew she was right. "But how can God forgive me for all I've done?" he asked himself one night. Premdas recalled Sunday school lessons and the prayer meetings held in his house when he was a boy.

"God," he whispered so no one could hear, "if You aren't real, I'm going to take my life. Are You real?"

A voice rang in his mind: "Son, I am the God you knew as a child. You are My child. I am your God."

Premdas swung his feet off the cot and sat up. "I believe, Lord. You *are* real. What do You want me to do?"

There was no response. He fell back asleep and had a dream unlike the nightmares that had plagued him for months. It was a dream he would never forget.

Answering God's Call

That Sunday he began attending church regularly. Mark Buntain's sermons from the Bible reminded Premdas of many of the stories he had heard as a boy.

Not many weeks later, Premdas walked to the front of the church and asked Mark to reintroduce him to Jesus Christ.

"What is your name?" Mark inquired after they had prayed the sinner's prayer.

"My name is Premdas. I have been coming to hear you speak about your God for several months."

Mark shook the young man's hand cordially and excused himself to pray for others who had come to the altar to accept Christ.

"But sir," Premdas spoke up, "before you go, can I ask you one question?"

"Sure, how can I help you?"

"God wants me to do what you are doing, to preach the Bible. But first I must learn more. Where can I learn?"

"How do you know God wants you to be a minister?"

"God told me in a dream."

"Oh, tell me about it."

"There was a balance scale, with a Bible on one side and many books on the other. I looked at the balance, and the Bible was much heavier, more important. That was God's way of telling me what I was to do with my life."

"Maybe it is, but you musn't wait until you are well-educated to tell your friends about what God has done for you."

Mark put his warm hand on the boy's arm and prayed with the stranger. "God, use this young man in a mighty way. Show him what You would have him do with his life. May he become a bold witness for You."

Premdas pondered Mark's advice in the hallway long after the minister had departed.

A week later, the one-time terrorist hiked back to his old community to tell his former neighbors and fellow gang members about Jesus. Word spread quickly of his transformation and devotion to Jesus Christ. Still, residents tried to elude the preacher.

At least, now, they no longer had to dodge Premdas out of fear for their lives. The young man was now more concerned with their souls.

CHAPTER THIRTEEN

Bijan

"Please bless my son," the woman squealed, falling at Bijan's feet. "He is very ill." She handed the religious man a basket of fruit. "Please take this as an offering."

The man stood upright in his saffron robe and leather thongs, his eyes feasting on the beautiful trees and hills surrounding him. The woman kissed the holy man's feet, awaiting the words that would heal her son. She could see that this small man had traveled many miles. The callouses on his feet were deforming. His hairline was receding on each side, making him appear much older than twenty-four.

Three years earlier, Bijan had taken the vow of the Sanyasi,* a nomadic lifestyle of self-denial. The young man had left his wife and family with only the robe on his back for what he deemed would

* *Sanyasi:* a holy man of the Hindu faith on a life-long pilgrimage in pursuit of truth.

be a lifetime journey to discover the root of knowledge. All his life Bijan's parents had taught him that knowledge brought salvation.

"Remember that our souls are part of God, son. There is no difference between our souls and God. Knowledge is strength. Men are weak because they have no knowledge of themselves," his parents often taught him.

Bijan lived in the shadow of trees, along dirt roads, seeking a revelation of himself. Streams spilling from the Ganges provided refreshment while peasant worshipers supplied nutritional sustenance.

When Bijan entered a hamlet, villagers welcomed him as a supreme holy man. Onlookers dropped to the ground in adoration; children rushed to touch his cotton garment. "The gods will bless our village today. A Sanyasi has come," they would say.

That evening, while lying inside a ditch along the national highway—a paved road that stretches from Delhi to Calcutta—Bijan slurped juice from an orange. He pulled his cotton skirt down over his feet to keep warm. The tips of the sun's rays sprayed above the mountains, casting a gloomy gray across the sky. Bijan meditated, peering inside his mind for a simple truth that would fill today's experiences with meaning.

Returning Home

His solitude suddenly turned to chaos as a vehicle screeched to a halt yards from his prone body. Friends he hadn't seen for years dismounted from an old British pickup. They had come to convince him to return to his wife, Lurani, the girl he had married at the age of thirteen. The little man urged his "kidnappers" to leave him alone as they encircled him.

"You must leave me now," Bijan ordered as the abductors stepped closer. "I cannot go with you."

In spite of his pleadings, the holy man was forced into the bed of the truck. He found himself speeding away without recourse. Riding in a motorized vehicle again felt peculiar. The excitable holy man reclined, resigned to the fact he was heading home.

In time, Bijan renounced his vow as a Sanyasi and turned to a teaching career. He earned a postgraduate degree and accepted a position as an instructor. Bijan's salary and influence in the community grew, along with a desire to partake of the pleasures he had sacrificed as a Sanyasi.

"Bijan, what will you drink?" the thin bartender asked.

"Whiskey," he said, plopping down on a swivel stool.

The invigorating music bounced off every wall. Behind Bijan, dancers hopped to the lively beat. Five swallows later, Bijan was on the dance floor. In between selections, he darted to the bar to be rejuvenated.

This evening would end like so many others, with Bijan asleep, his cheek pasted to the top of the bar. Fortunately, his wife always knew where to find him.

A Dismal Diagnosis

The scholar was still unhappy. Self-denial and, subsequently, self-indulgence had left him dissatisfied. He scoured religious books searching for a phrase, a word, a solution to his struggle for happiness. Lurani slept while Bijan lay awake at night gleaning from the most prolific passages of world philosophy. She would often awaken only to find him asleep, hugging the pages of a book.

"You must come to bed," Lurani suggested one evening, seeing that Bijan was engrossed in another book.

"I cannot. This has merit. I'll come to bed later," he said.

It was nearly dawn when Bijan noticed a twinge in his back. It must be from sitting so long, he thought. The pain, however, persisted. Some days he could not crawl from his mattress. His lower spine felt like it was in a vice grip. Sleeping became nearly impossible. Each movement struck a nerve.

Lurani finally convinced him to have his back examined by a doctor. For an instant, Bijan blamed his wife for the physician's diagnosis: "A malignant tumor on your backbone." Bijan pounded his fist into the arm of his chair without saying a word. Lurani and the doctor could feel his anguish. The young wife pried open his clenched fist and inserted her soft hand. The rings on her fingers were cold, yet her hands were warm against his sweating palms.

"Is there nothing we can do?" the woman asked, exploring the doctor's face for a glimmer of hope.

The doctor closed the file in front of him. "I wish . . ." he hesitated. "I wish there was something I could tell you."

"Is there somewhere we can take him?" she asked.

"I'm sorry." The doctor bowed his head.

Bijan sat quietly, searching the chronicles of philosophy in his mind for a solution. He said nothing during the rickshaw ride home. Lurani honored his silence.

Days passed, and he rarely spoke. She knew he was trying to be courageous, to display an inner strength enamored by the gods. Nevertheless,

Lurani could not accept her husband's death. It was a nightmare she refused to watch.

Self-Imposed Exile

The curried vegetables were cooling on Bijan's plate, untouched. Lurani said nothing.

"I must leave this place," said Bijan matter-of-factly.

Lurani did not object. "I'll go with you."

"I am dying. There is nothing you can do. Please, let me have my pride. Let me die alone."

"You cannot leave me again," she insisted, shaking her head. "I must go with you."

Bijan stood from the table. "I will not permit it. Your family is here. This is where you belong. I will have it no other way," he ordered.

"Please, do not leave me," Lurani begged.

"I do not want you to suffer with me. This is how it must be. You will have a good life here. I cannot. I don't want my friends to see me die. I must go far from here to Calcutta."

Bijan's train snaked its way through the mountains, from village to town. Wild animals retreated from the rail as the train approached. Shallow watering holes and green bushes lined the tracks. At every station Bijan, perched on a slightly bent metal seat, eyed even the most decrepit person through his window with envy.

If only I could have been you, and you me, he repeated in his mind.

Passengers evaded a man whose face and arms were covered with boils. The man sat alone in the crowded compartment. Bijan, too, turned his head to avoid the sight.

Maybe I shouldn't go to Calcutta, he thought. Maybe I should return to the countryside where no one will have to see my body deteriorate. But the thought of vultures and maggots feasting on his corpse ended further deliberation.

The ride from Calcutta's train station to the hostel where he would stay was enough to diminish his self-pity. The sights were deplorable. Children were scooping brown water into cups. Flies were fluttering above seemingly lifeless bodies on the pavement, occasionally landing to rest their wings.

"God Can Heal You"

Once Bijan arrived at the hostel and got situated, he felt better. At least I will die in a soft bed, he thought. The hostel, his citadel, provided no more than a cot in a room with twenty strangers. It was there, however, that Bijan met a local priest.

"God can heal you," Father Haselton said.

"Have you ever seen anyone healed?"

"No, Bijan, I have not."

Bijan was disappointed. "Then how do you know He can?"

"The Bible says He can," the priest noted. "Read the Bible—especially the gospels. You'll see for yourself."

In college, Bijan had often scoffed at Christians for their beliefs and efforts to convert unbelievers. His classmates united behind him, denouncing Christians as deceived, witless creatures. Now, in his desperate state, he found himself reading the Bible, particularly the life of Christ and the many healings He performed.

"Jesus," he prayed each day, his face buried under his blanket as he grimaced in pain. "If You are the most powerful God, heal me. Show me Your power. If You choose to heal me, I will give my life to You."

Residents of the hostel, faithful to their Eastern religion, challenged the validity of Bijan's prayers. Moreover, some were angered by the presence of his Bible.

"Surely a man of your background cannot believe the Bible," a young man scoffed.

"You're not a Christian are you?" another declared.

Bijan knew the severity of his disease had driven him to the Bible, but he hoped this God could remove his tumor anyway. He began attending a Christian church and learning more about this Savior he was praying to—Jesus Christ.

"I Must Be Baptized Now!"

As the weeks passed, Bijan's faith grew. The pain in his back had intensified as well. Despite his agony, he found himself defending Christ in debates with his roommates. Then one evening the prayer he had recited each day changed.

"Dear God, I believe You are real and that You can heal me. Even if You choose not to, I will still believe." His heavenly conversation lasted for hours. It was four o'clock, and the hostel was tranquil except for the faint sound of snoring of a temporary resident.

In a flurry, Bijan dashed out into the crisp night air. He hurdled a few beggars and trotted through the gates of the church he had attended. His knuckles bashed against the intricately sculptured wooden door. Father Haselton, only half awake, answered.

"Yes," the Caucasian minister yawned.

"Father, I received Christ tonight. Will you baptize me?"

The minister rubbed his eyes. "Yes, Bijan, I will baptize you," he said with all the excitement he could muster. "Come this afternoon. I will be waiting."

"Thank you, Father, but I must be baptized now."

The minister rubbed his eyes again, hoping he'd heard wrong. "Now?" he asked.

"Yes!" Bijan smiled.

"I'm afraid I don't understand. Can't it wait?"

"No, Father, it must be now." The minister waved the small man inside.

Growing in Faith

Bijan's decision to be baptized as a Christian was met with deep remorse by his family. The letters from his wife ceased, and financial assistance from his family no longer arrived. Despite his sickness, Bijan was forced to seek employment.

Jobs were scarce. But a school principal, impressed with Bijan's credentials, scheduled an interview on a Sunday to discuss an opening on their faculty. To the principal's astonishment, Bijan refused to meet on "God's day" and therefore forfeited the job. Friends at the hostel thought Bijan's illness had affected his brain.

"It's only one Sunday. A job is more important than church," they reasoned.

"I must go to church. God will provide another job."

Indeed, while Bijan was at church that very Sunday, another headmaster delivered a job offer to the hostel. As a result, Bijan's faith was bolstered, and it served as a testimony to his friends.

A few days later, he also noticed the pain in his back diminishing.

"I know God has healed my back," he announced to his roommates. "The pain is going away."

His companions were cautious. "Go see a doctor. He will tell you if it's true."

"I need no doctor. I am healed. I believe Jesus has healed me."

The roommates at the hostel were now certain their friend had experienced a mental lapse of some kind.

"Surely he can't believe *Jesus* has done this," they muttered behind his back.

Bijan knew they were questioning his sanity, but he wasn't perturbed. He was just grateful to be feeling healthy again.

Some months later, Bijan accepted a new job and began attending Mark Buntain's church. Upon hearing of his recovery, Lurani came to Calcutta. Although she was grateful her husband's disease had gone into remission, she was displeased with his new religious beliefs. She often threatened to leave Bijan unless he denied his faith in Christ. She despised his prayers and loyalty to the church, often spewing insults at him as he departed for Royd Street.

Lurani, meanwhile, set her idols and candles in the front room where she knelt daily to pray that the gods would reveal her husband's foolishness to him.

Whenever Bijan returned from work, he could smell the sharp fragrance of the incense and candles.

"You must not perform these rituals in this house," he demanded.

"Then you cannot read your Bible," she said firmly. The arguments persisted for many months before Bijan sought Mark's counsel.

Surrounded by Angels

One afternoon, when Bijan quietly stepped into Mark's office, he witnessed a scene that left him speechless. The preacher was praying silently at his desk, his hands covering his face. The room was brightly lit. Five glowing figures hovered around Mark. Bijan quietly backed out of the room.

An hour later he returned to Mark's office, his eyes opened wide with excitement. "Pastor, I came in earlier today when you were praying."

"You should have let me know, Bijan."

"No, Pastor, there were angels praying with you. I couldn't disturb you."

Mark wasn't sure what it was the man had seen, and thus, redirected the conversation. "Thank you, Bijan, for being so considerate. What can I do for you?"

The man hesitated at first. "Pastor, I'm having arguments with my wife. She is an unbeliever. She is against my religion. What can I do?"

Mark leaned back. The top of his tie was hidden under his chin. "You musn't argue with her. That doesn't accomplish anything. Love her. Show her Christ is in you."

"But she doesn't believe it was Christ who healed me. She thinks it was *her* prayers."

Mark tilted forward. "You know those angels you said you saw?"

Bijan nodded.

"Well, you have angels watching over you, too. Did you know that? They're with you in your house. They're with us now. Believe me, together with Jesus, they are going to protect you and your home from the enemy. Let them take care of that. Just love her."

Bijan walked into his house that evening and wrapped his arms around his wife's waist.

"I love you," he whispered. Lurani didn't respond. "I love you so much," he repeated.

Tears formed in the outside corners of Lurani's eyes. She couldn't say anything. But it didn't matter. Bijan could almost see the angels applauding above his wife's images in the corner of the room. He could only smile, for Bijan knew one day she too would respond to the compelling voice of her Savior Jesus Christ.

The Assembly of God Hospital and Research Center in Calcutta.

Postscript

Huldah Buntain set the phone down in her hotel room in Bangkok, Thailand. She had just learned that Mark had suffered a massive cranial hemorrhage.

The following morning she was to fly to the States to be with her daughters and grandchildren. Instead she found herself rushing to the airport to secure a return flight to Calcutta. Sometime later, while waiting in the airport terminal, she received another telephone message—this time from long-time associate and friend, the Reverend Ronald Shaw.

"Huldah, Mark's gone to be with the Lord," he said.

Sunday, June 4, 1989, at approximately 9:00 a.m., Mark went to his heavenly home. He was sixty-six years old.

Hours after his death, the tragic news had already swept around the world. Announcers on Christian television and radio and pastors from their pulpits reported Mark's death to their listeners.

Several days later, religious leaders and friends boarded jetliners to attend the funeral services in Calcutta or one of the memorial proceedings in Tacoma, Washington, and Columbia, Missouri.

In Calcutta, hundreds walked behind the hearse as it made its way down Royd Street. Weeping bystanders lined the side of the street. The procession stopped in front of Mark's original church and school. There, a government official laid a wreath on his casket, for this is where it all started.

The hearse then traveled to Park Street where the hospital, new church, school, and offices are located, and where Mark was to be buried. The news media reported as many as 12,000 were in attendance.

Throughout the service, tears flowed from the orphaned children Mark had rescued, the sickly he had helped, and the pastors he had trained. They had lost a spiritual father and leader. But Mark gave them more than food, medical care, and an education; he gave them the answer to eternal life with their heavenly Father.

Mark's compassion is legendary, and the highrise hospital, Bible college, and feeding program he established are monumental; but his greatest legacy is that he "laid down his life for his friends." And now Calcutta will never be the same.

Huldah is now the pastor and Chairman of the Board, and she has vowed to continue the work she and her husband started more than thirty years ago. May God continue to guide her as He did her husband.

Associate Pastor Ron Shaw leads worship at the Assembly of God Church in Calcutta, which was pastored by Mark Buntain for over thirty years.

About the Authors

Fulton Buntain is the pastor of the 5,000 member First Assembly of God Life Center in Tacoma, Washington. He hosts the weekly television programs "Introduction to Life" and "Hour of Life." He has authored numerous booklets and received an honorary doctorate from Northwest College

Hal Donaldson served as editor of ON Magazine and taught at Bethany Bible College. He is the president of The ChurchCare Network, an organization that sends ministries—at no cost—to smaller churches. He has written other books, including *Where is the Lost Ark?* and *Treasures in Heaven*—the life story of Huldah Buntain.

Other material about Mark Buntain and the Calcutta Mission of Mercy:

Books

The Compassionate Touch

Mark

Films and Videos

Calcutta Mission of Mercy

Oh How Much Jesus Loves You

If Our Gospel is Hid

To Light a Candle

Mark Speaks to Children

For more information concerning books, films, videos, and the work of the Calcutta Mission of Mercy, write:

Calcutta Mission of Mercy
P. O. Box 11108
Tacoma, WA 98411-9985